Houghton
Mifflin
Harcourt

CALIFORNIA
MATH
Expressions
Common Core

Dr. Karen C. Fuson

GRADE

K

Volume 1

This material is based upon work supported by the
National Science Foundation
under Grant Numbers
ESI-9816320, REC-9806020, and RED-935373.

Any opinions, findings, and conclusions, or recommendations expressed in this material
are those of the author and do not necessarily reflect the views of the National Science Foundation.

VOLUME 1 CONTENTS

UNIT 1 Understand Numbers 1–10

BIG IDEA 1   Counting and Cardinality 1–5

BIG IDEA 2   Adding, Subtracting, and Comparing Through 5

* This lesson consists only of activities from the Teacher Edition.

VOLUME 1 CONTENTS *(continued)*

* This lesson consists only of activities from the Teacher Edition.

* This lesson consists only of activities from the Teacher Edition.

UNIT 3 Teen Numbers as Tens and Ones

* This lesson consists only of activities from the Teacher Edition.

© Houghton Mifflin Harcourt Publishing Company

* This lesson consists only of activities from the Teacher Edition.

Family Letter

Content Overview

Dear Family:

Your child is learning math in an innovative program that weaves abstract mathematical concepts with the everyday experiences of children. This helps children understand math better.

Your child will have homework. He or she needs a **Homework Helper**. The helper may be anyone—you, an older brother or sister (or other family member), a neighbor, or a friend. Make a specific time for homework and provide your child with a quiet place to work (for example, no TV). Encourage your child to talk about what is happening in math class. If your child is having problems with math, please talk to the teacher to see how you might help.

Thank you! You are vital to your child's learning.

Sincerely,
Your child's teacher

- -

Please fill out the following information and return this form to the teacher.

My child _____Navya_____ will have _____
(child's name) (Homework Helper's name)

as his or her Homework Helper. This person is my child's

_____.
(relationship to child: father,
mother, sibling, friend, etc.)

Estimada familia:

Su niño está aprendiendo matemáticas con un programa innovador que relaciona conceptos matemáticos abstractos con la experiencia diaria de los niños. Esto ayuda a los niños a entender mejor las matemáticas.

Su niño tendrá tarea y necesita a una persona que lo ayude. Esa persona puede ser usted, un hermano mayor (u otro familiar), un vecino o un amigo. Establezca una hora para la tarea y ofrezca a su niño un lugar tranquilo donde trabajar (por ejemplo un lugar sin TV). Anime a su niño a comentar lo que está aprendiendo en la clase de matemáticas. Si su niño tiene problemas con las matemáticas, por favor hable con el maestro para ver cómo usted puede ayudar.

Muchas gracias. Usted es imprescindible en el aprendizaje de su niño.

Atentamente,
El maestro de su niño

- -

Por favor complete la siguiente información y devuelva este formulario al maestro.

La persona que ayudará a mi niño _____ es
(nombre del niño)

_____ . Esta persona es _____
(nombre de la persona)   (relación con el niño)

de mi niño.

Introduce Number and Counting Routines

1	2	3	4	5	6
1	**2**	**3**	**4**	**5**	**6**

7	8	9	10
7	**8**	**9**	**10**

Number Tiles and Square-Inch Tiles **3**

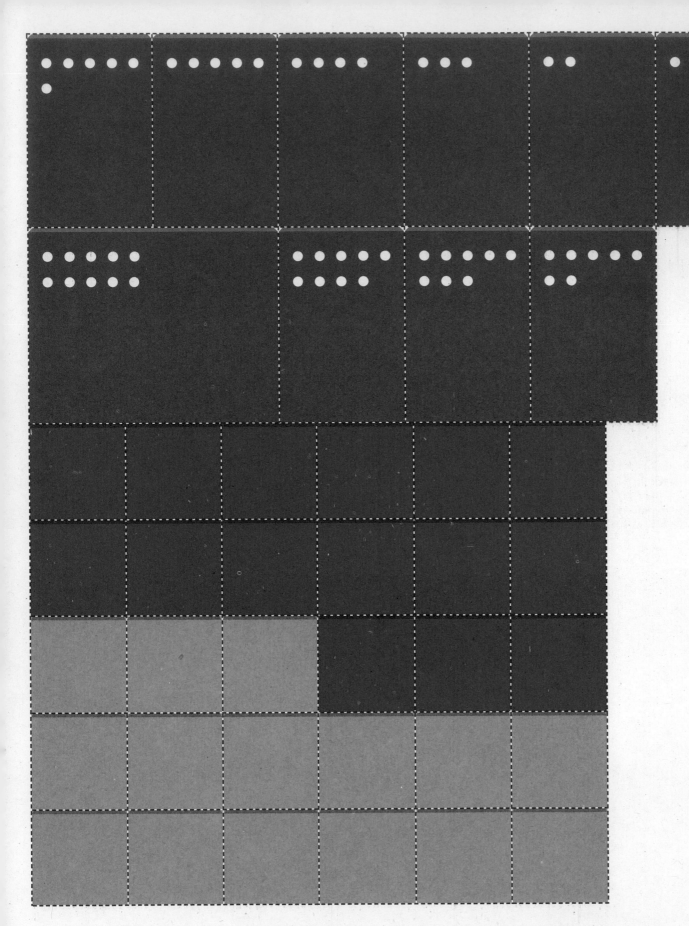

Number Tiles and Square-Inch Tiles

Dear Family:

Your child has just read and discussed *Anno's Counting Book*. This book is an introduction to beginning numbers. It is filled with charming scenes that show many things all of the same number (for example, a scene showing many different groups of 3 things). Each page shows a month of the year.

We have discussed what a scene is in class. *A scene is a place where some action or event occurs, a picture.* The children will be making their own scenes or pictures. Sometimes this will be started in class and completed for homework. You can help by talking with your child about what he or she might draw, for example, your child might draw 2 of something, such as things found in a kitchen—2 plates, 2 bowls, 2 spoons.

Help your child practice counting things in daily life. Children might count how many stairs there are in your home, how many plates you need to set the table, or how many people are in the family.

Thank you for helping your child learn more about numbers and counting!

Sincerely,
Your child's teacher

CA CC

Unit 1 addresses the following standards from the *Common Core State Standards for Mathematics with California Additions*: **K.CC.1, K.CC.2, K.CC.3, K.CC.4a, K.CC.4b, K.CC.5, K.CC.6, K.OA.1, K.OA.2, K.MD.3, K.G.1, K.G.2, K.G.3, K.G.4, K.G.5** and all Mathematical Practices.

Estimada familia:

Su niño acaba de leer y comentar un libro para contar. Este libro es una introducción a los primeros números. Está lleno de escenas fascinantes que muestran muchas cosas, todas acerca de los mismos números (por ejemplo, una escena muestra varios grupos diferentes de 3 cosas). Cada página indica un mes del año.

Hemos comentado en clase lo que es una escena. *Una escena es un lugar donde ocurre una acción o un suceso, un dibujo.* Los niños van a hacer sus propias escenas o dibujos. A veces los empezarán en clase y los terminarán de tarea. Usted puede ayudar hablando con su niño sobre lo que puede dibujar. Por ejemplo: si va a dibujar 2 de algo, podría dibujar cosas que están en la cocina, 2 platos, 2 tazones, 2 cucharas.

Ayude a su niño a practicar contando cosas que usen a diario. Los niños pueden contar cuántas escaleras hay en su casa, cuántos platos se necesitan para poner la mesa o cuántas personas hay en la familia.

¡Gracias por ayudar a su niño a aprender más sobre los números y a contar!

Atentamente,
El maestro de su niño

© Houghton Mifflin Harcourt Publishing Company

CA CC

En la Unidad 1 se aplican los siguientes estándares auxiliares, contenidos en los *Estándares Estatales Comunes de Matemáticas con Adiciones para California*: **K.CC.1, K.CC.2, K.CC.3, K.CC.4a, K.CC.4b, K.CC.5, K.CC.6, K.OA.1, K.OA.2, K.MD.3, K.G.1, K.G.2, K.G.3, K.G.4, K.G.5** y todos los de prácticas matemáticas.

Name Navya

CA CC Content Standards K.CC.4a, K.CC.4b
Mathematical Practices MP.3, MP.7

Draw 5 hats.

Draw 3 cats.

Draw 4 stars.

Draw 2 cars.

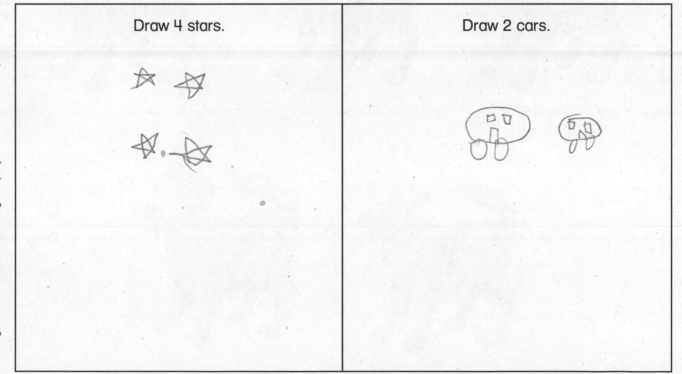

Name Navyo

Look at what Puzzled Penguin wrote.

Help Puzzled Penguin.

6 dogs   No

5 dogs

Am I correct?

_5_ dogs

Scenes and Visual Imagery

Circles

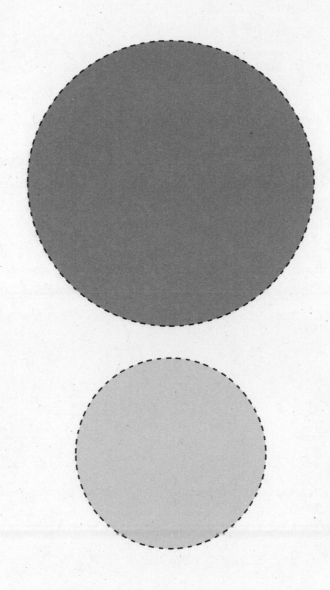

Circles

Name _____

CA CC Content Standards K.G.1, K.G.2, K.G.4, K.G.5
Mathematical Practices MP.1

Trace the **circles**.
Color the circles.

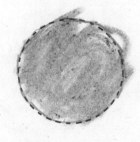

Look at the red circle.

Draw two circles that are larger.

Draw two circles that are smaller.

Color the circles different colors.

Identify Circles

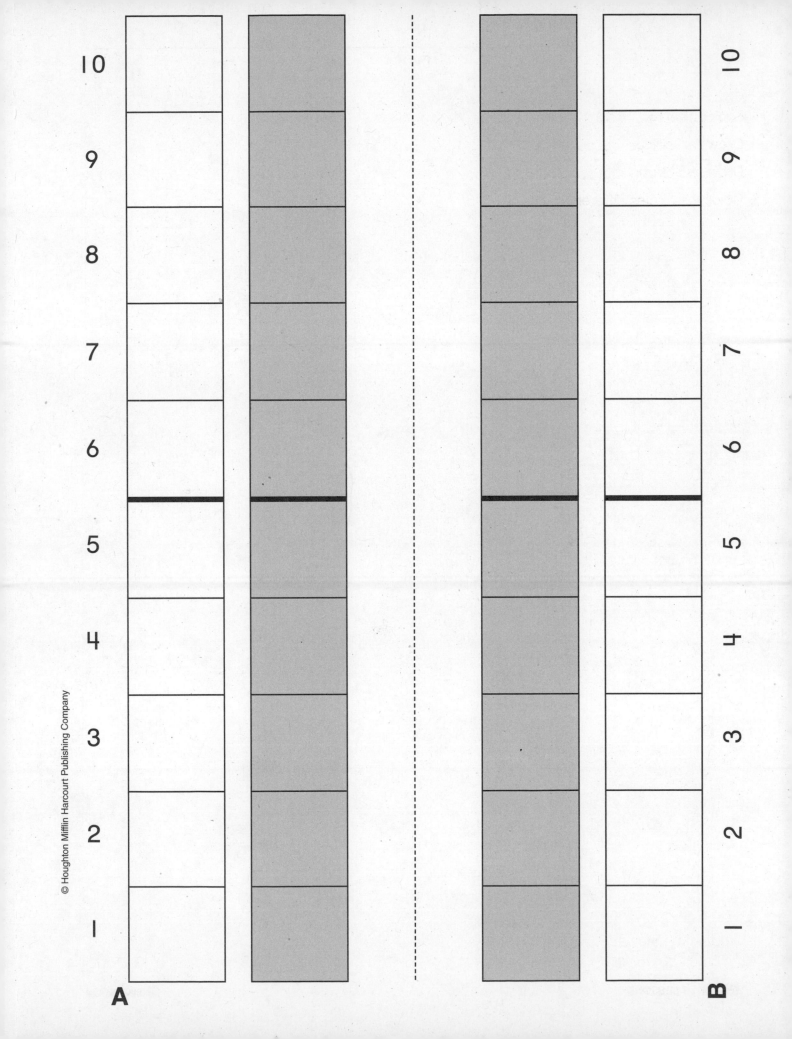

A

10   9   8   7   6   5   4   3   2   1

B

10   9   8   7   6   5   4   3   2   1

Comparing Mat

Squares and Rectangles

Squares and Rectangles

Name

CA CC Content Standards **K.MD.3, K.G.2**
Mathematical Practices **MP.3, MP.6**

Color the **circles** yellow. Color the **squares** blue.
Draw a face under your favorite hat.

Name _____

VOCABULARY
circle, square,
rectangle

Color each kind of shape.

circle   square   rectangle

Dear Family:

Your child is learning to write numbers. You might notice that sometimes your child might write numbers backwards or reverse them. This is very common in early number writing. You can ask your child, "Does this number look OK?" Then point out that it is written backwards. Eventually our goal is that children may identify their own reversals, write correct numbers, and write faster in preparation for first grade.

Thank you!

Sincerely,
Your child's teacher

 CA CC

Unit 1 addresses the following standards from the *Common Core State Standards for Mathematics with California Additions*: **K.CC.1, K.CC.2, K.CC.3, K.CC.4a, K.CC.4b, K.CC.5, K.CC.6, K.OA.1, K.OA.2, K.MD.3, K.G.1, K.G.2, K.G.3, K.G.4, K.G.5** and all Mathematical Practices.

Estimada familia:

Su niño está aprendiendo a escribir los números. Usted observará que a veces su niño escribe los números al revés o que los invierte. Esto es normal al empezar a escribir los números. Puede preguntarle, "¿Está bien escrito este número?" Luego indíquele que está escrito al revés. Nuestro objetivo es que, más adelante, los niños se den cuenta de que han invertido los números, que los escriban correctamente y que escriban más rápido para prepararse para el primer grado.

¡Gracias!

Atentamente,
El maestro de su niño

CA CC

En la Unidad 1 se aplican los siguientes estándares auxiliares, contenidos en los *Estándares Estatales Comunes de Matemáticas con Adiciones para California*: **K.CC.1, K.CC.2, K.CC.3, K.CC.4a, K.CC.4b, K.CC.5, K.CC.6, K.OA.1, K.OA.2, K.MD.3, K.G.1, K.G.2, K.G.3, K.G.4, K.G.5** y todos los de prácticas matemáticas.

Name _____

CA CC Content Standards **K.CC.3, K.CC.4a, K.CC.4b**
Mathematical Practices **MP.6**

Write the numbers.

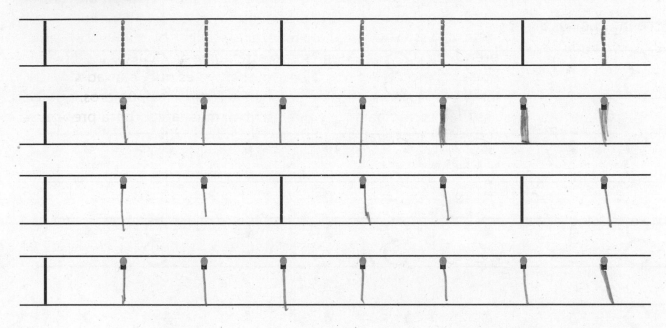

VOCABULARY
circles

Write the number 3.

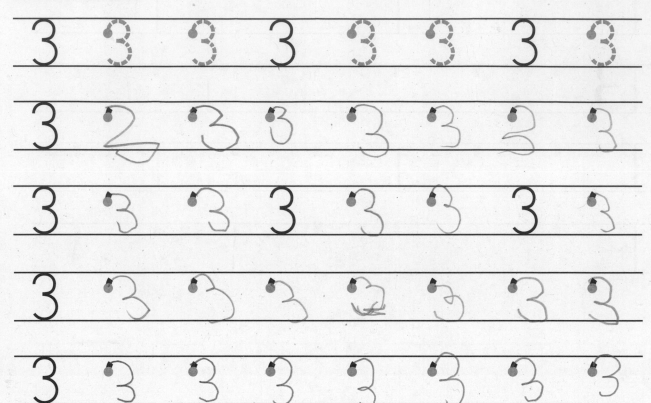

Draw 3 objects.	Draw 3 **circles**.

CA CC Content Standards **K.CC.3, K.CC.4a, K.CC.4b, K.CC.5**
Mathematical Practices **MP.6**

Go left to right. Ring **groups** of the number. Mark an X on the groups that are not the number.

3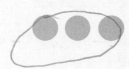

4

5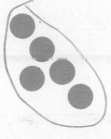

2

Name Navya Garg

3 3 3 3 3 3 3 3

3 3 3 3 3 3 3 3

3 3 3 3 3 3 3 3

3 3 3 3 3 3 3 3

Practice Numbers I—I0

Name

CA CC Content Standards K.CC.3, K.CC.4a, K.CC.4b, K.OA.1, K.OA.2 Mathematical Practices MP.2, MP.4, MP.6, MP.8

Write the number 4.

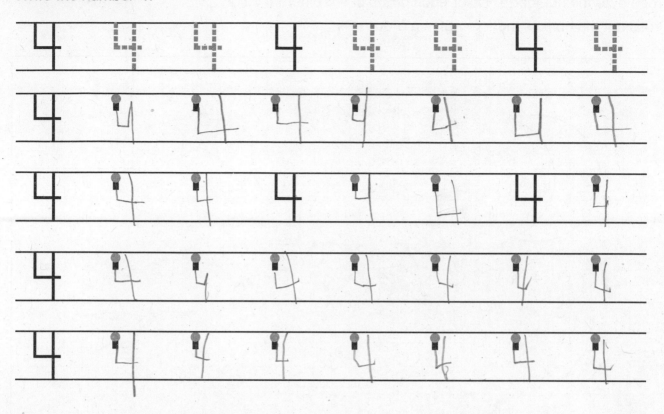

Draw 4 objects.

Draw 4 rectangles.

Trace over the number 4. Color each group of 4 a different color.

Cross out the objects that are not in a group of 4.

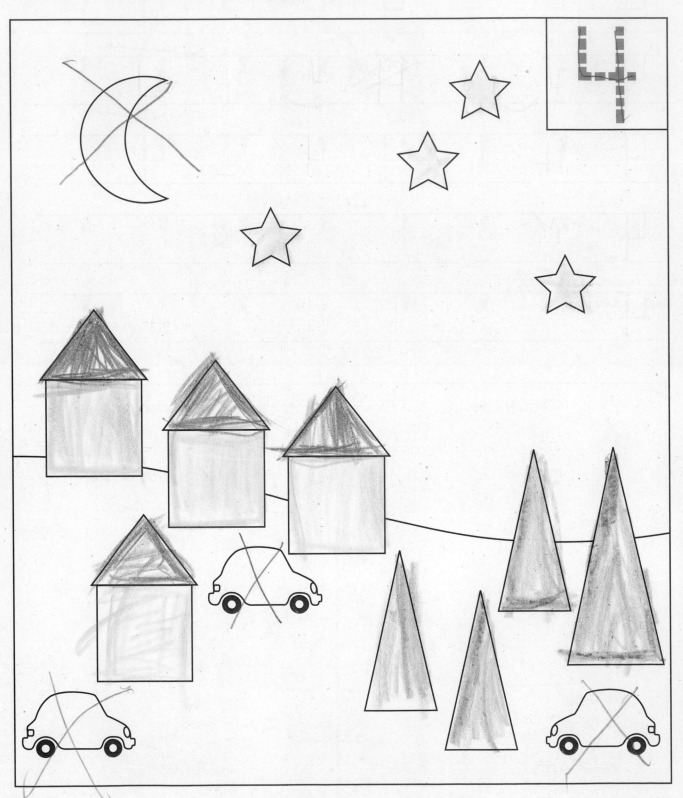

Numbers of Objects in a Group

Tell an adding story.

	First	Then	At the end

1.

2.

Tell a subtracting story.

	First	Then	At the end

3.

4.

Tell math stories about the pictures.

5.

6.

7.

8.

Numbers of Objects in a Group

Name

CA CC Content Standards K.CC.4a, K.CC.4b, K.CC.5, K.CC.6, K.CC.7
Mathematical Practices MP.3, MP.6

Puzzled Penguin compared numbers.

Puzzled Penguin showed the numbers.

Then Puzzled Penguin drew a circle around
the number that is greater. Help Puzzled Penguin.

Am I correct?

No

Yes

⑥ 8

⑨ 7

Go left to right. Ring groups of the number. Mark an X on the groups that are not the number.

3

 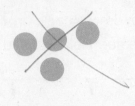 

4

 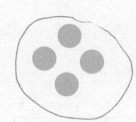 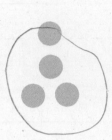 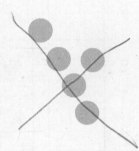

5

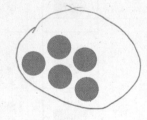 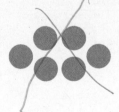 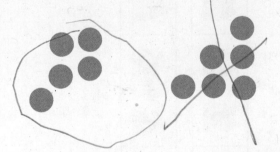

2

Objects and Numbers Through 10

Name _____

CA CC Content Standards **K.CC.3, K.CC.4a, K.CC.4b, K.CC.5, K.CC.6** Mathematical Practices **MP.2, MP.6**

Write the number 5.

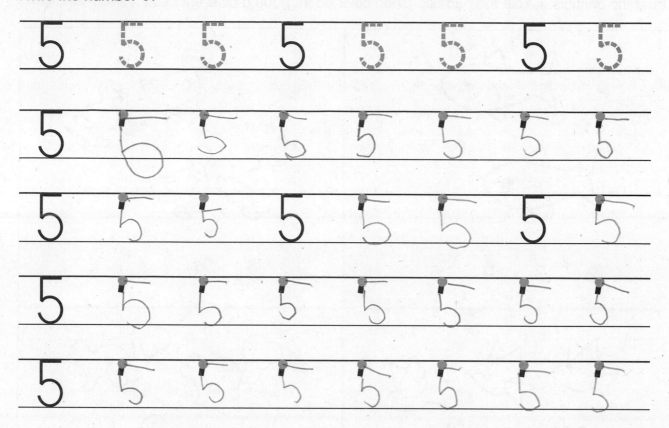

Draw 5 objects.	Draw 5 squares.
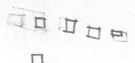	

Name _____

Count the animals. Circle the number. Then color each group a different color.

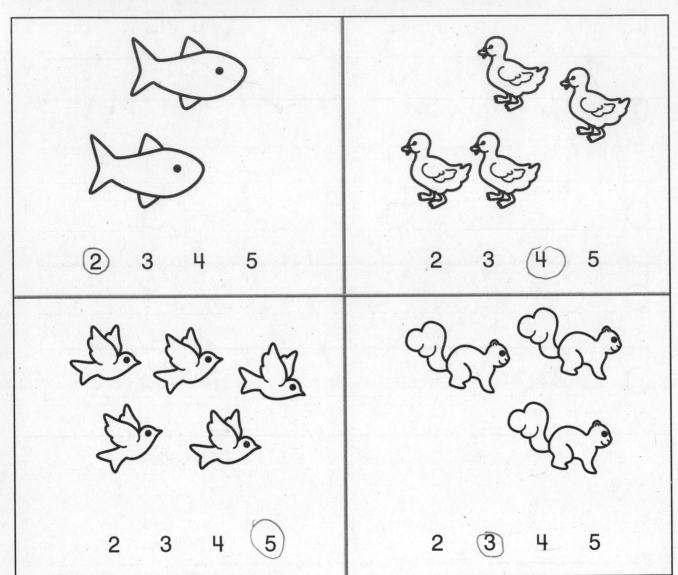

Write the number 0.

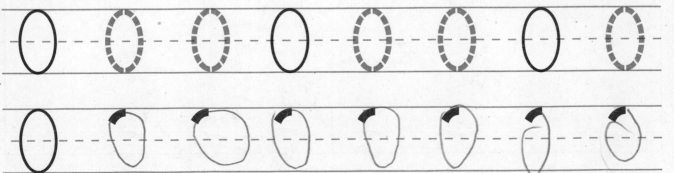

Practice: Number of Objects in a Group

Name

CA CC Content Standards K.CC.1, K.CC.3
Mathematical Practices MP.6, MP.8

Connect the dots in **order**.

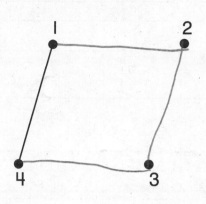

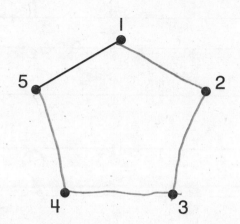

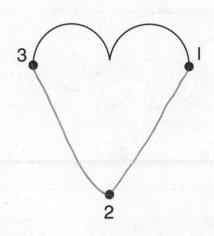

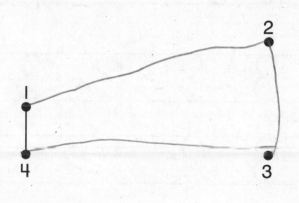

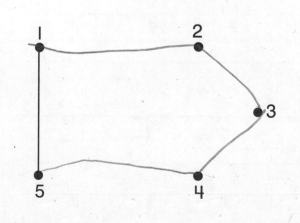

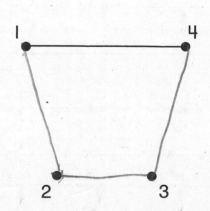

Name

Write the numbers.

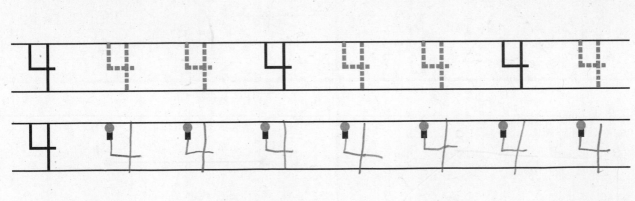

1   1   1   1   1   1   1   1

2   2   2   2   2   2   2   2

2   2   2   2   2   2   2   2

3   3   3   3   3   3   3   3

3   3   3   3   3   3   3   3

4   4   4   4   4   4   4   4

4   4   4   4   4   4   4   4

5   5   5   5   5   5   5   5

5   5   5   5   5   5   5   5

More Objects and Numbers Through 10

Name

CA CC Content Standards K.G.2, K.G.3, K.G.4, K.G.5
Mathematical Practices MP.1, MP.4, MP.5, MP.6, MP.7, MP.8

Color shapes with no straight sides blue.

Color shapes with 4 sides red.

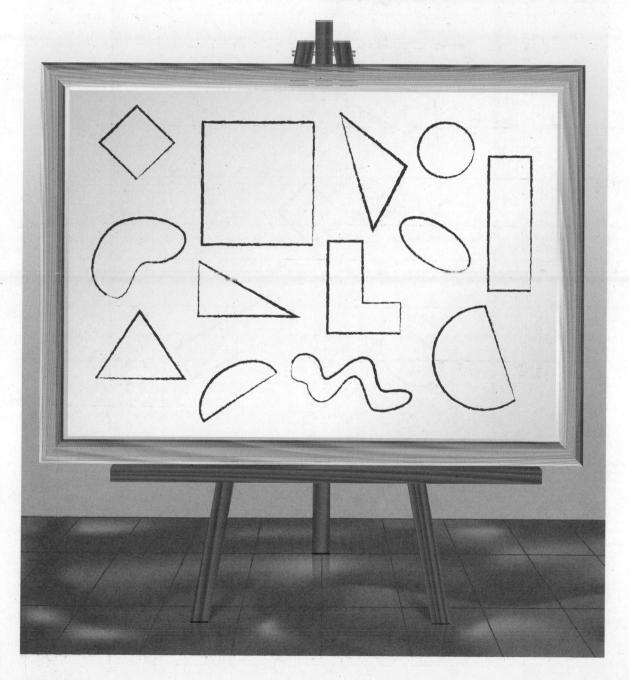

Draw some shapes with no straight sides.

Draw some shapes with 4 sides.

Focus on Mathematical Practices

Ring groups of the number. Mark an X on the groups that are not the number.

1.

2.

 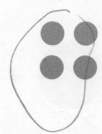   

---

3. Draw 3 trees.

4. Draw 5 flowers.

5. Draw a line under each circle.

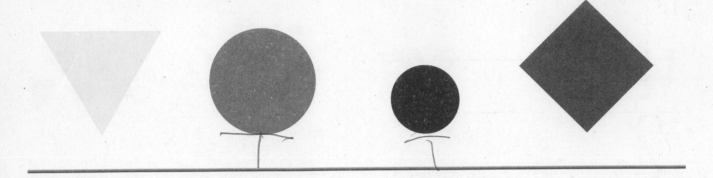

6. Draw a line under each rectangle.

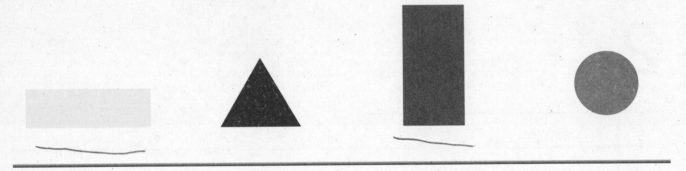

7. Connect the dots in order.

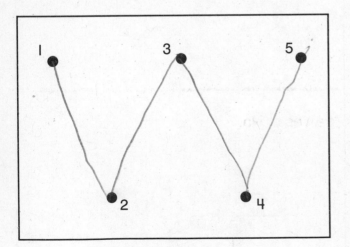

8.

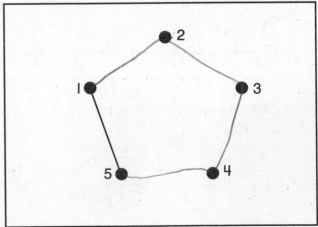

9. Write the numbers.

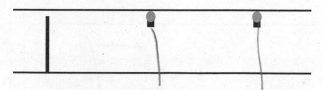

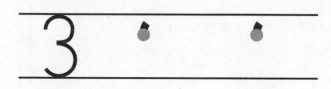

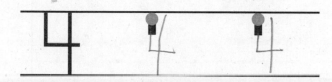

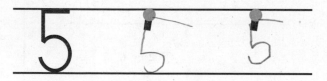

10. Does the picture match the number? Choose Yes or No.

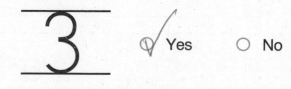

3   ✓ Yes   ○ No

11. Make a drawing. Use 1 square, 3 circles, and 4 rectangles. Did you draw fewer squares or circles? Mark an X on the shape that has fewer.

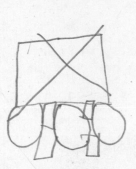

Family Letter

Content Overview

Dear Family:

Children are learning to see numbers 6, 7, 8, 9, and 10 as having a 5 and some more. This is called using a 5-group. This visual pattern will help children add, subtract, and understand numbers. It will also help later in multidigit calculation.

Count things at home in 5-groups to help your child see the 5 in 6, 7, 8, 9, and 10. For example, 7 buttons can be counted using 5-groups: "5 and 2 make 7."

Children will see 5-groups in materials they are using in school:

Number Parade

6 7 8 9 10

Square-Inch Tiles

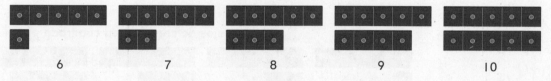

6   7   8   9   10

Counters and 5-Counter Strips

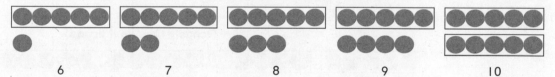

6   7   8   9   10

Thank you!

Sincerely,
Your child's teacher

 CA CC

Unit 2 addresses the following standards from the *Common Core State Standards for Mathematics with California Additions*: **K.CC.1, K.CC.2, K.CC.3, K.CC.4, K.CC.4a, K.CC.4b, K.CC.4c, K.CC.5, K.CC.6, K.CC.7, K.OA.1, K.OA.2, K.OA.3, K.OA.4, K.OA.5, K.MD.3, K.G.1, K.G.2, K.G.4,** and all Mathematical Practices.

Estimada familia:

Los niños están aprendiendo a ver que los números 6, 7, 8, 9 y 10 contienen el 5 y algo más. Esto se llama usar un grupo de 5. Este patrón visual los ayudará a sumar, a restar y a entender los números. Más adelante también les servirá para los cálculos con números de más de un dígito.

Cuenten cosas en casa haciendo grupos de 5 para que el niño identifique el 5 en el 6, 7, 8 , 9 y 10. Por ejemplo, pueden contar 7 botones haciendo un grupo de 5: "5 más 2 son 7".

Los niños identificarán grupos de 5 en los materiales que usan en la escuela:

Desfile de números

6 7 8 9 10

Azulejos de una pulgada cuadrada

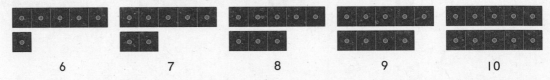

6   7   8   9   10

Fichas y tiras de 5 fichas

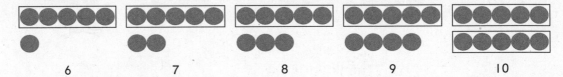

6   7   8   9   10

¡Muchas gracias!

Atentamente,
El maestro de su niño

© Houghton Mifflin Harcourt Publishing Company

 CA CC

En la Unidad 2 se aplican los siguientes estándares auxiliares, contenidos en los *Estándares Estatales Comunes de Matemáticas con Adiciones para California*: **K.CC.1, K.CC.2, K.CC.3, K.CC.4, K.CC.4a, K.CC.4b, K.CC.4c, K.CC.5, K.CC.6, K.CC.7, K.OA.1, K.OA.2, K.OA.3, K.OA.4, K.OA.5, K.MD.3, K.G.1, K.G.2, K.G.4** y todos los de prácticas matemáticas.

Name _____

CA CC Content Standards **K.CC.3, K.CC.5**
Mathematical Practices **MP.1, MP.3, MP.6**

Find groups of 1 through 10.

Help Puzzled Penguin.

Did Puzzled Penguin write the numbers
1 through 10 in order correctly?

Yes

1	2	3	4	6	5	7	8	9	10

Write the numbers 1 through 10 in order.

1	2	3	4	5	6	7	8	9	10

Write the numbers 0 through 9 in order.

0	1	2	3	4	5	6	7	8	9

Cut on dashed lines.
Do not cut on solid lines.

5-Square Tiles **45**

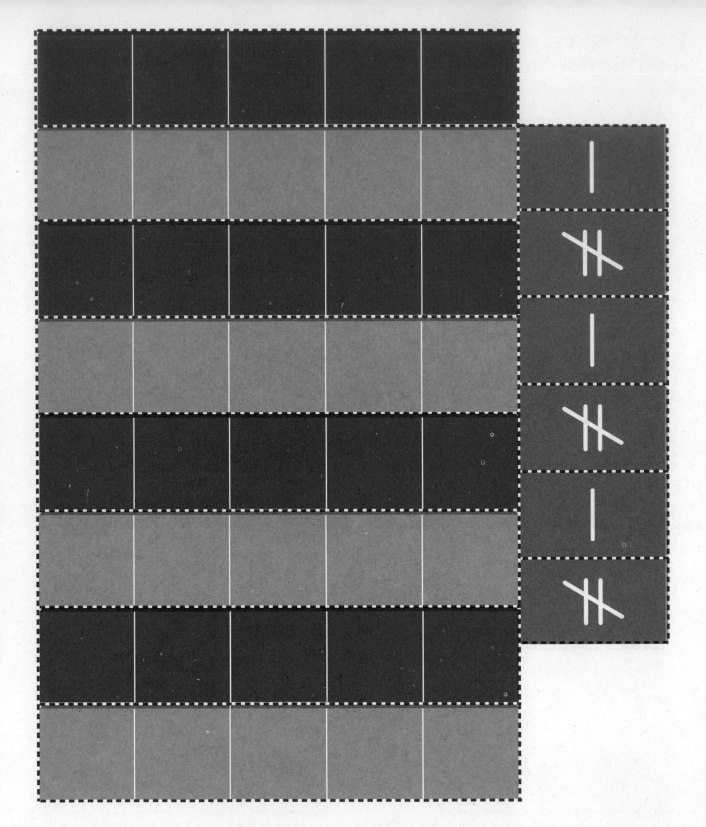

Ring groups of the number. Cross out groups that are not the number.

6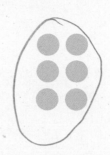

7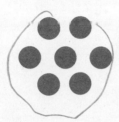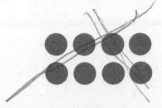

8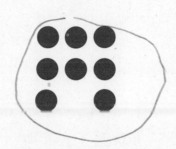

9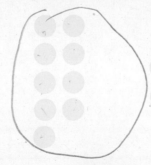

10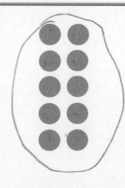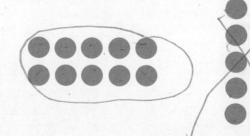

Draw dots to show the number.

6

_____

7

_____

8

_____

9

_____

10

Family Math Stories

Cut on dashed lines. **Fold** on solid lines and tape at top and bottom.

5

5

5

5

5

5

Write the number 6.

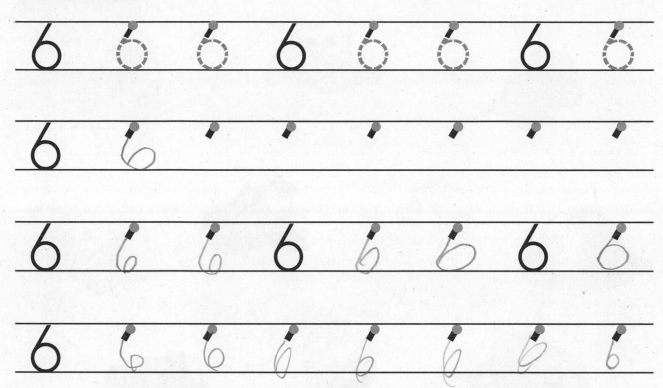

Draw 6 objects.	Draw 6 balls.
0 0 0 0 0 0	

Ring 6 hats.

Write the number 6.

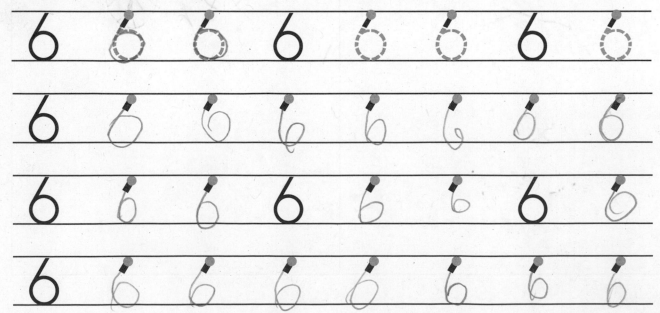

Add and Subtract with Family Math Stories

Name

CA CC Content Standards **K.CC.1, K.OA.1, K.OA.2, K.OA.5** Mathematical Practices **MP.1, MP.6**

Tell an addition or subtraction story.

Make a drawing to show how many balloons in all.

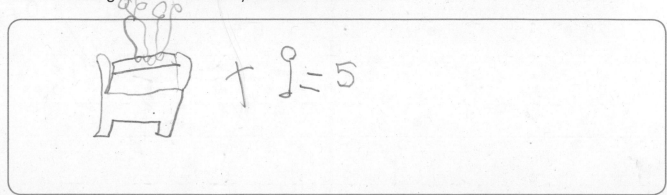

VOCABULARY
straight lines

Connect the dots in order. Use **straight lines**.

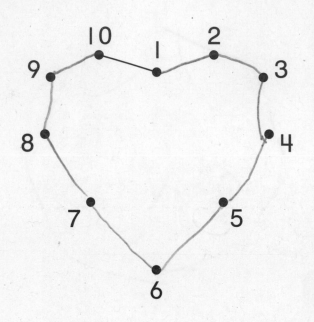

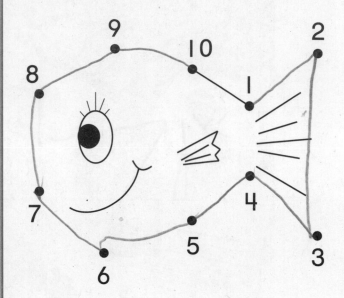

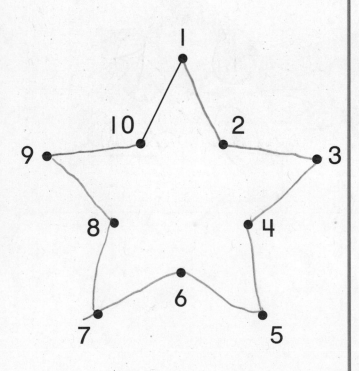

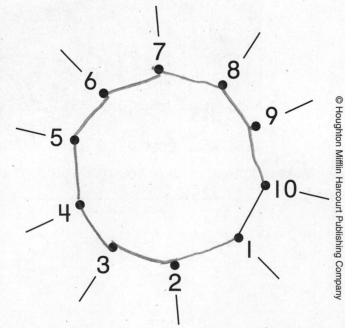

Addition and Subtraction Stories: Playground Scenario

1	2	3	4	5	6
1	2	3	4	5	6

7	8	9	10
7	8	9	10

=	+	=	+	=	+
=	+	=	+	=	+

+ / − Tiles, = / ≠ Tiles

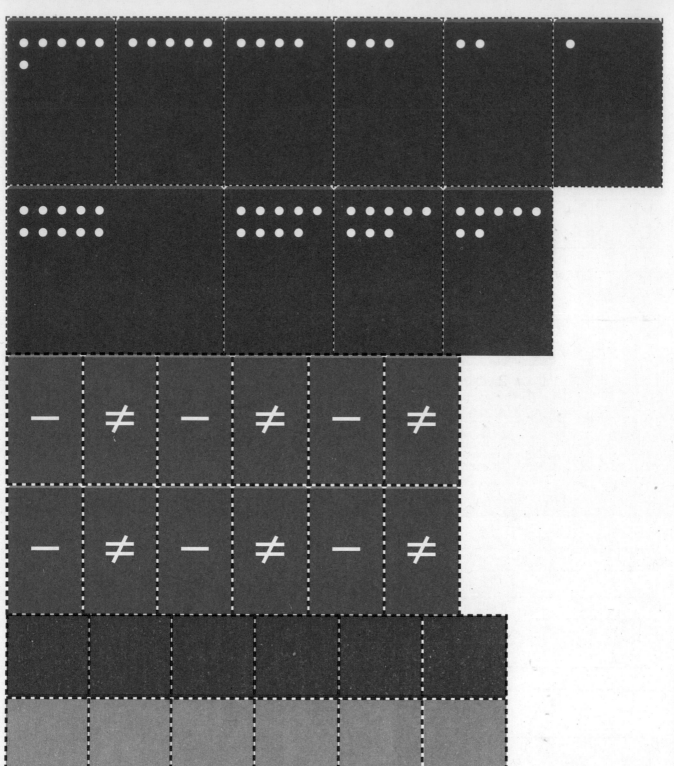

$+/-$ Tiles, $=/\neq$ Tiles

CA CC Content Standards K.CC.1, K.CC.3, K.CC.5
Mathematical Practices MP.6

Name _____

Write the numbers 2 and 5.

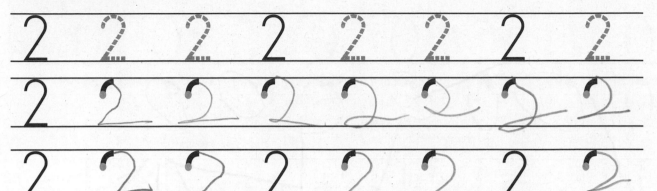

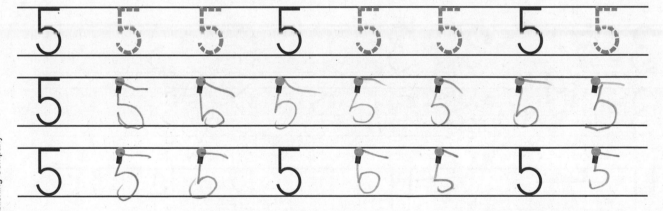

Draw 2 objects.	Draw 2 circles.

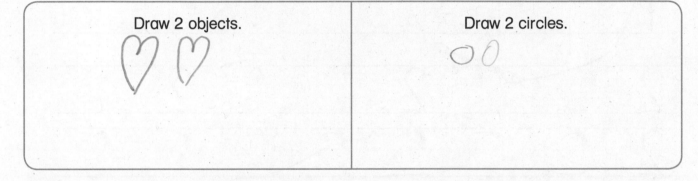

Draw 5 objects.	Draw 5 squares.

Write numbers 0 through 5 in order. Use the Number Parade to help.

0   0   0   0   0   0   0   0

0   0   0   0   0   0   0   0

1   1   1   1   1   1   1   1

1   1   1   1   1   1   1   1

2   2   2   2   2   2   2   2

2   2   2   2   2   2   2   2

3   3   3   3   3   3   3   3

3   3   3   3   3   3   3   3

4   4   4   4   4   4   4   4

4   4   4   4   4   4   4   4

5   5   5   5   5   5   5   5

5   5   5   5   5   5   5   5

Numbers 6–10

CA CC Content Standards **K.CC.1, K.CC.3, K.CC.4a, K.CC.5** Mathematical Practices **MP.1, MP.6, MP.7**

Write the number 7.

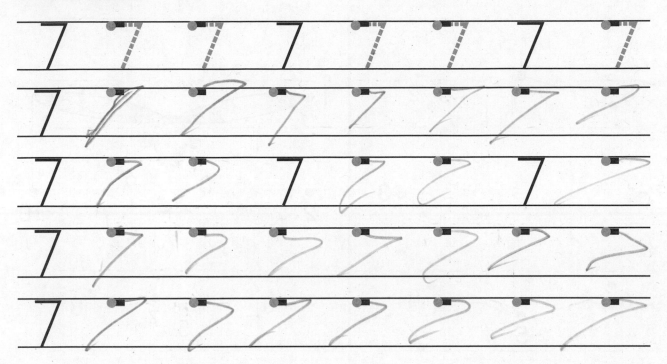

Draw 7 objects.	Draw 7 squares.

Write the numbers 0 through 7 in order.

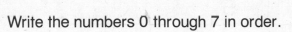

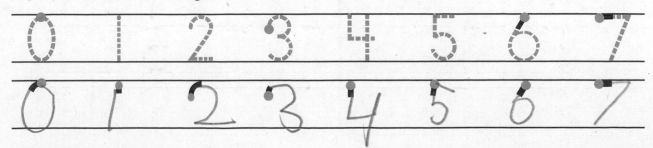

© Houghton Mifflin Harcourt Publishing Company

Connect the dots in order.

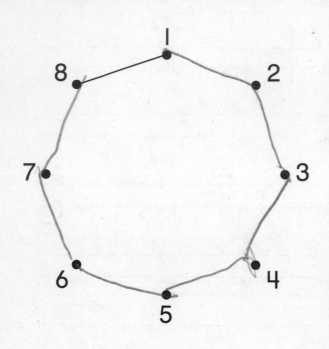

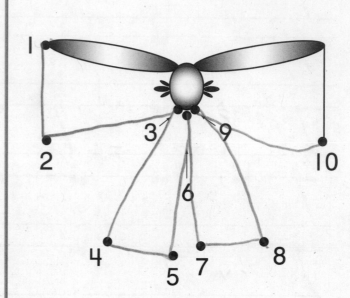

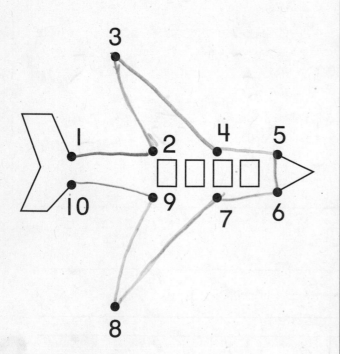

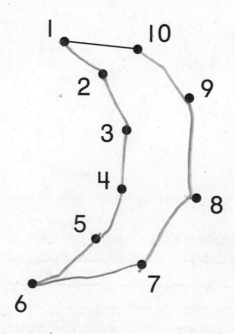

Numbers 1–10

Use a pencil or marker and trace each number
2 times. Use the color blue to trace the 6s and
the color red to trace the 7s.

| 6 | ● ● ● ● ● ● |
| 7 | ● ● ● ● ● ● ● |

Write the numbers 1 through 7 in order.

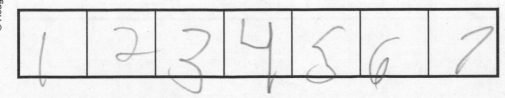

| 1 | 2 | 3 | 4 | 5 | 6 | 7 |

Help Puzzled Penguin.

Did Puzzled Penguin make a mistake?

Look at the numbers below.

Did I make a mistake?

yes

| 7 | 6 | 9 | 10 | 8 |

Write the numbers 6 through 10 in order.

| 6 | 7 | 8 | 9 | 10 |

Write the numbers 1 through 10 in order.

| 1 | 2 | 3 | 4 | 5 | 6 | 7 | 8 | 9 | 10 |

Practice with 5-Groups

Name

CA CC Content Standards **K.CC.3, K.CC.4a, K.CC.4b, K.CC.5** Mathematical Practices **MP.6**

Write the number 8.

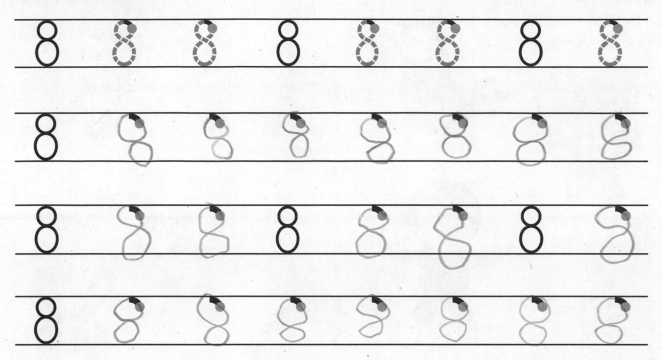

Draw 8 objects.	Draw 8 rectangles.

Ring 8 objects.

Write the number 8.

8 8 8 8 8 8 8 8

8

8 8

8

Numbers 6, 7, and 8

Tell a math story.

The Neighborhood GARDEN

Write the number 9.

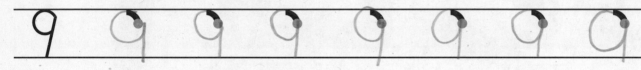

Draw 9 objects.	Draw 9 triangles.

Addition and Subtraction Stories: Garden Scenario

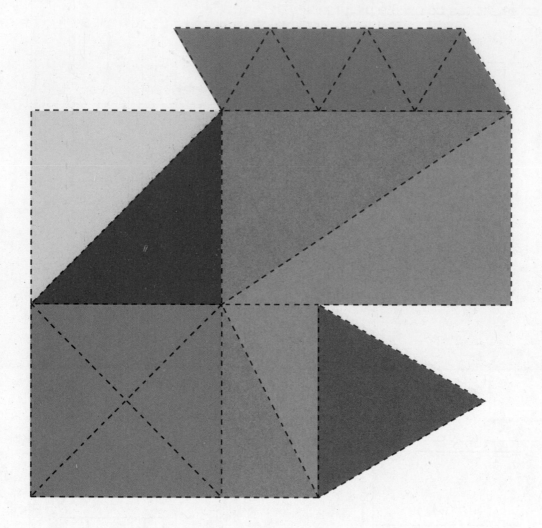

Triangles

Name

CA CC Content Standards **K.G.1, K.G.2**
Mathematical Practices **MP.1, MP.6, MP.7**

Discuss shapes you see.

Trace the shapes.

Draw the same shapes below the pictures.

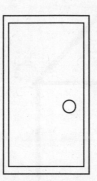

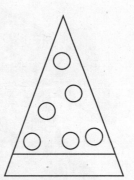

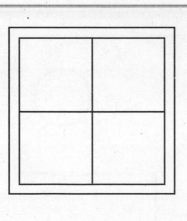

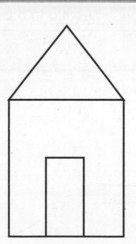

Name shapes you see.

Count the sides of each shape.

Color each shape needed to build the dog house above.

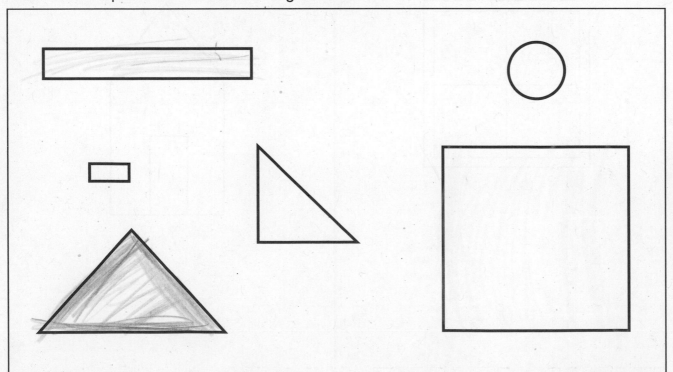

Identify Triangles

Write the number 10.

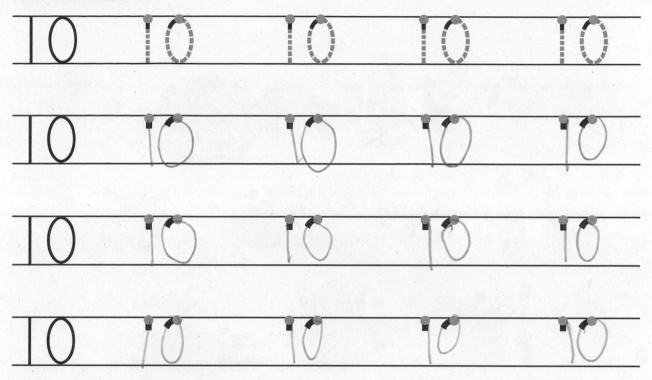

Draw 10 objects.	Draw 10 circles.

Ring 10 fish.

Practice writing the number 10.

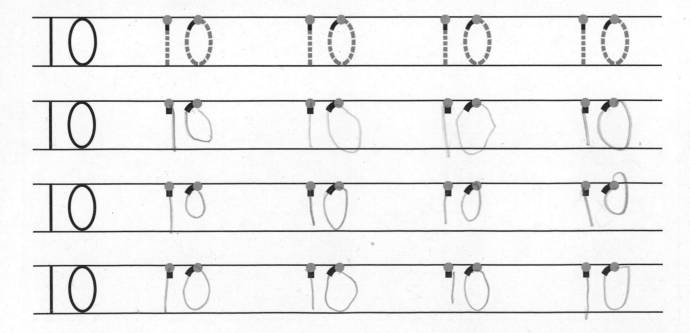

Addition and Subtraction Stories: Family Experiences

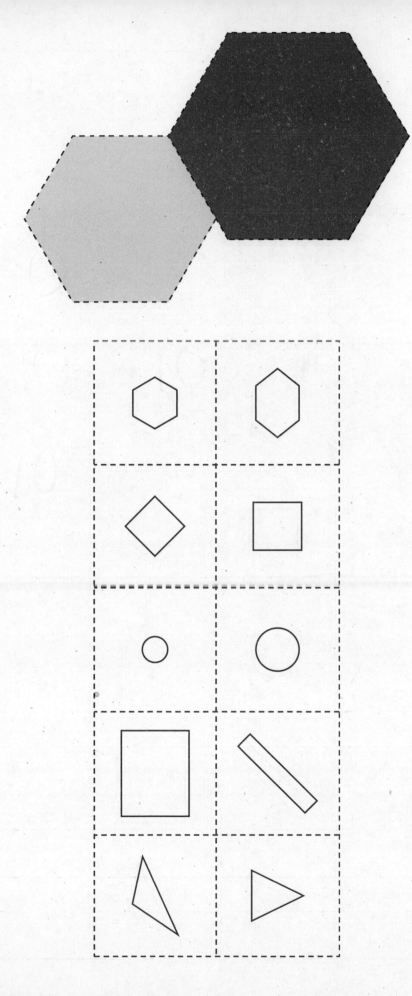

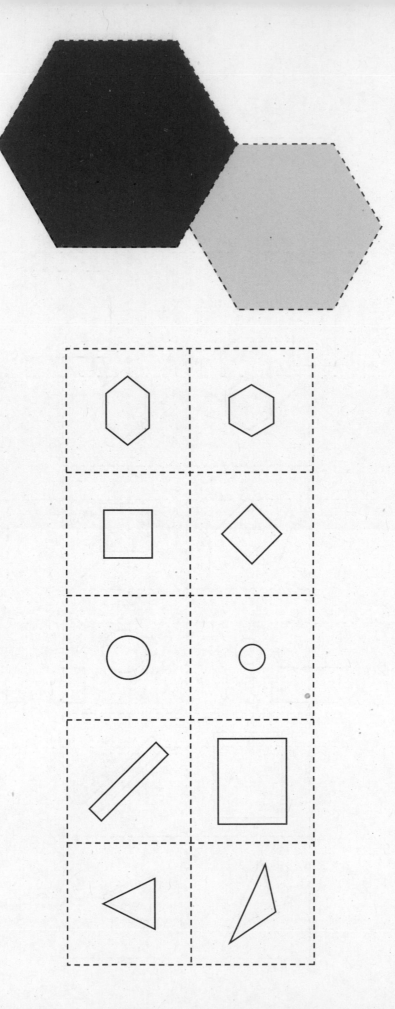

Hexagons

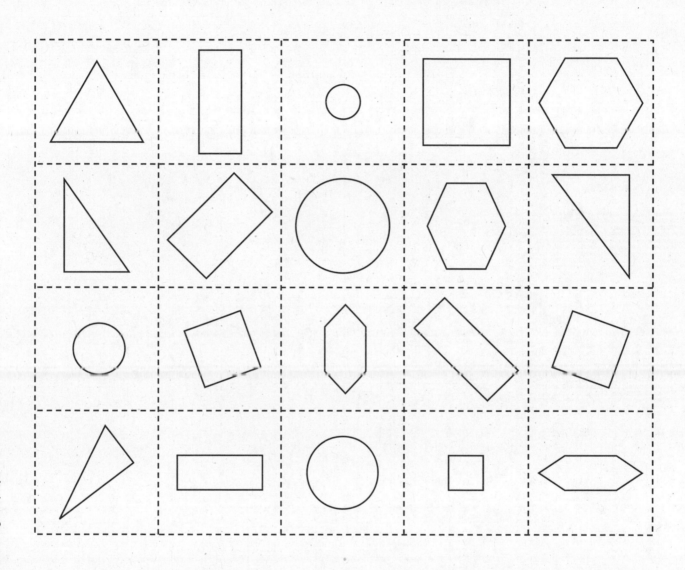

Identify Hexagons **75**

Identify Hexagons

Name _____

CA CC Content Standards K.MD.3, K.G.1, K.G.2, K.G.4
Mathematical Practices MP.3, MP.6

Color the shapes of one kind the same color as below.

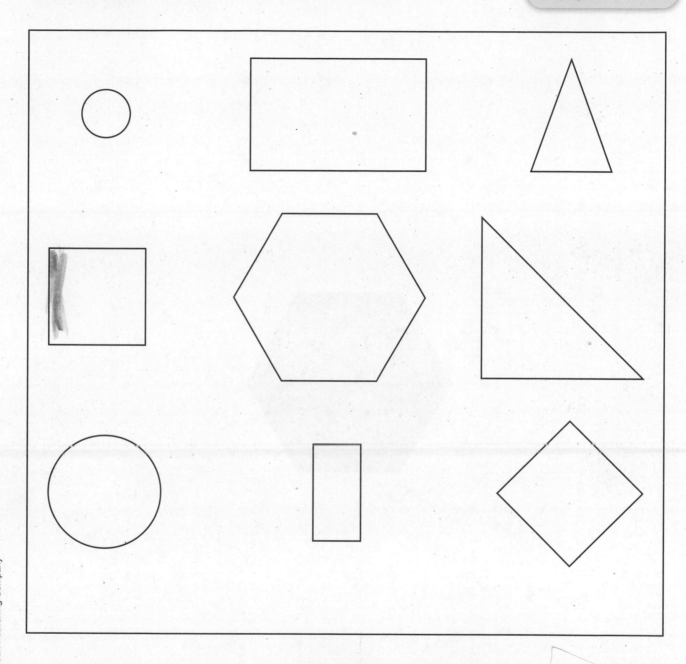

circle

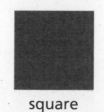
triangle

square

hexagon

rectangle

Name _____

Identify Hexagons

Use a pencil or marker.

Trace each number two times.

Use the color red to trace the 8s.

Use the color blue to trace the 9s.

Write the numbers 1 through 10 in order.

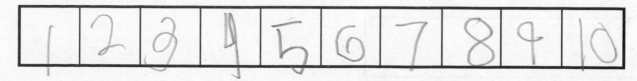

1	2	3	4	5	6	7	8	9	10

Name _____

Help Puzzled Penguin.

Puzzled Penguin was asked to write the number 6.

Did Puzzled Penguin write the number correctly?

Am I correct?

What number did Puzzled Penguin write?

How can we help Puzzled Penguin write the correct number?

Write the number for Puzzled Penguin.

Practice writing the number 6.

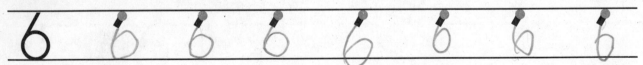

Practice writing the number 9.

Write the numbers 6 through 10 in order.

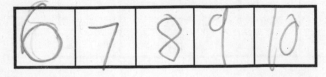

Number Writing Practice

Help Puzzled Penguin.

Did Puzzled Penguin make a mistake?

Look at the numbers below.

Did I make a mistake?

yes

Cross out any numbers that are not in the correct order.

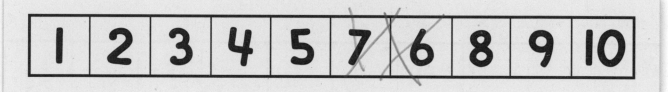

1 2 3 4 5 7 ~~6~~ 8 9 10

Help Puzzled Penguin write the numbers in the correct order.

| 1 | 2 | 3 | 4 | 5 | 6 | 7 | 8 | 9 | 10 |

Cross out any numbers that are not in the correct order.

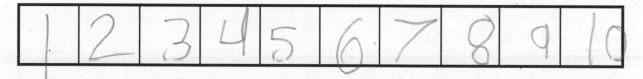

0 1 2 3 4 5 6 7 9 ~~8~~

Help Puzzled Penguin write the numbers in the correct order.

| 0 | 1 | 2 | 3 | 4 | 5 | 6 | 7 | 8 | 9 |

Write the numbers 1 through 10 in order.

| 1 | 2 | 3 | 4 | 5 | 6 | 7 | 8 | 9 | 10 |

| 1 | 2 | 3 | 4 | 5 | 6 | 7 | 8 | 9 | 10 |

| 1 | 2 | 3 | 4 | 5 | 6 | 7 | 8 | 9 | 10 |

Write the numbers 0 through 9 in order.

| 0 | 1 | 2 | 3 | 4 | 5 | 6 | 7 | 8 | 9 |

| 0 | 1 | 2 | 3 | 4 | 5 | 6 | 7 | 8 | 9 |

| 0 | 1 | 2 | 3 | 4 | 5 | 6 | 7 | 8 | 9 |

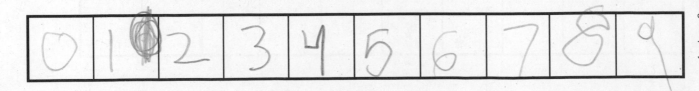

More Numbers 1 Through 10: The −1 Pattern

Color the shapes of one kind the same color.

Count the number of each shape.

Write the number.

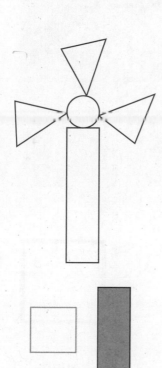

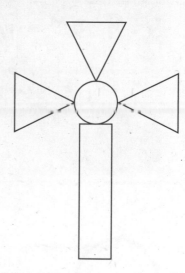

Name

Draw a line to match each shape below to a shape in the picture.

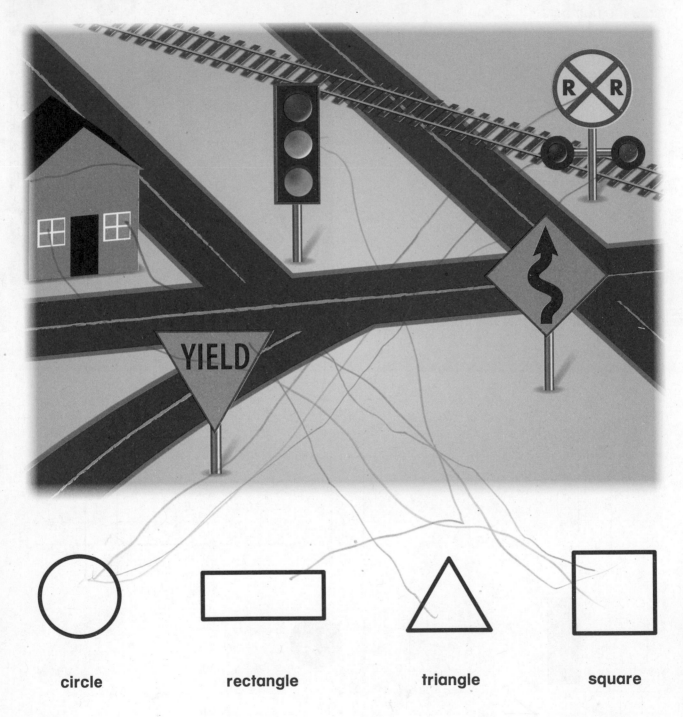

circle   rectangle   triangle   square

Focus on Mathematical Practices

1. Choose all the groups of the number.

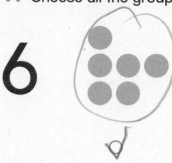  

6

○̸ ○ ○̸

2. Does the set show 7? Choose Yes or No.

○̸ Yes ○ No

○̸ Yes ○ No

○ Yes ✗ No

Connect the dots in order.

3.

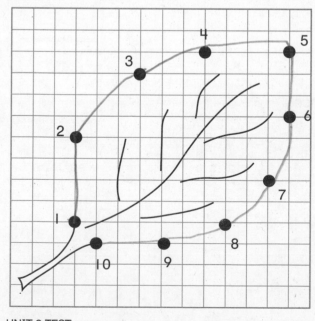

4.

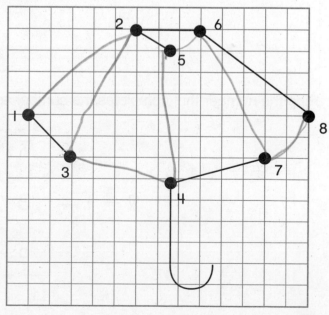

Name

5. Ring the 5-group. Count the total. Write the number.

$$5 + 1 = \boxed{6}$$

---

6. There are 9 circles. Draw a set of circles that shows 9 — 1.

Ring the number that completes the number sentence.

$$9 - 1 = \begin{array}{|c|} 7 \\ \boxed{8} \\ 9 \end{array}$$

7. Draw 4 triangles in the box. Write how many sides a triangle has.

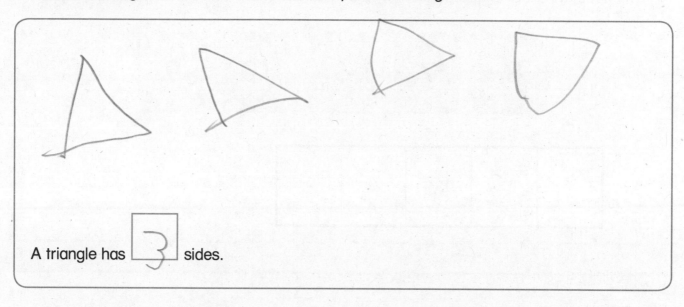

A triangle has ⎡3⎤ sides.

---

8. Draw a line under each hexagon.

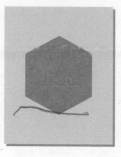   

9. Look at the number tiles. Write the numbers 6 through 10 in order.

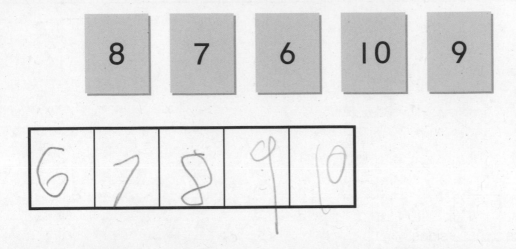

| 8 | 7 | 6 | 10 | 9 |

| 6 | 7 | 8 | 9 | 10 |

10. Draw a picture that shows 6 + 1 triangles.

Write how many triangles.

7

Dear Family:

Your child is starting a new unit on grouping concepts. These concepts provide a foundation for understanding basic math equations. In class, children will learn to find the ten in teen numbers ($17 = 10 + 7$), break apart numbers to find "partners" ($6 = 4 + 2$), recognize when numbers are equal or unequal, apply the concepts of *more* and *fewer*, and observe different attributes of shapes.

Being able to group numbers and shapes makes them easier to understand. You can help your child by practicing grouping concepts at home. Here is an example of an activity you can do with your child:

When cleaning up from play, have your child sort the objects before putting them away. Talk about the differences in size, shape, and color, and help your child place the items in groups based on these attributes. For example, the blocks below are sorted by size. They could also be sorted by color.

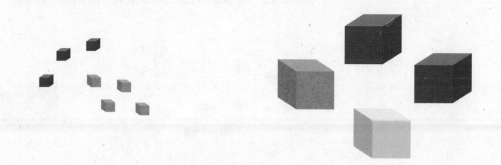

Thank you for your continued support.

Sincerely,
Your child's teacher

CA CC

Unit 3 addresses the following standards from the *Common Core State Standards for Mathematics with California Additions*: **K.CC.1, K.CC.2, K.CC.3, K.CC.4, K.CC.4a, K.CC.4b, K.CC.4c, K.CC.5, K.CC.6, K.CC.7, K.OA.1, K.OA.2, K.OA.3, K.OA.5, K.NBT.1, K.MD.3, K.G.1, K.G.2, K.G.4, K.G.6,** and all Mathematical Practices.

Estimada familia:

Su niño está empezando una nueva unidad que trata sobre los conceptos de agrupar. Estos conceptos son muy importantes para comprender las ecuaciones matemáticas básicas. Los niños aprenderán a hallar la decena en los números de 11 a 19 (17 = 10 + 7), a separar números para hallar "partes" (6 = 4 + 2), a reconocer si los números son iguales o no, a aplicar los conceptos de *más* y *menos* y a observar las características de las figuras.

Agrupar números y figuras facilita su comprensión. Usted puede ayudar a su niño practicando en casa los conceptos de agrupar. Aquí tiene un ejemplo de una actividad que pueden hacer:

Cuando estén guardando las cosas después de jugar, pida a su niño que separe los objetos en categorías. Háblele de las diferencias de tamaño, forma y color, y ayúdelo a colocar los objetos en grupos según estas características. Por ejemplo, los bloques que aparecen a continuación están agrupados según su tamaño. También se pueden agrupar según su color.

Gracias por su apoyo.

Atentamente,
El maestro de su niño

CA CC

En la Unidad 3 se aplican los siguientes estándares auxiliares, contenidos en los *Estándares Estatales Comunes de Matemáticas con Adiciones para California*: **K.CC.1, K.CC.2, K.CC.3, K.CC.4, K.CC.4a, K.CC.4b, K.CC.4c, K.CC.5, K.CC.6, K.CC.7, K.OA.1, K.OA.2, K.OA.3, K.OA.5, K.NBT.1, K.G.1, K.G.2, K.G.4, K.G.6** y todos los de prácticas matemáticas.

Name _____

CA CC Content Standards **K.CC.1, K.CC.3, K.CC.5, K.OA.2** Mathematical Practices **MP.1, MP.2, MP.3, MP.4, MP.6**

Color each group of 1 through 10 a different color.

1. Connect the dots in order.

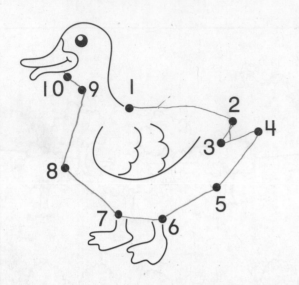

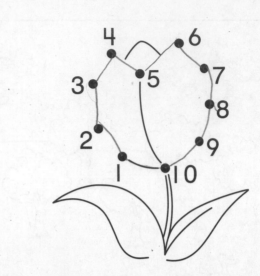

2. Help Puzzled Penguin.

Look at Puzzled Penguin's numbers.

Did Puzzled Penguin write the numbers in order?

Am I correct?

No

1	2	4	3	5	6	7	8	9	10

Write the numbers 1 through 10 in order.

1	2	3	4	5	6	7	8	9	10

Numbers 1–10 and Math Stories: Park Scene

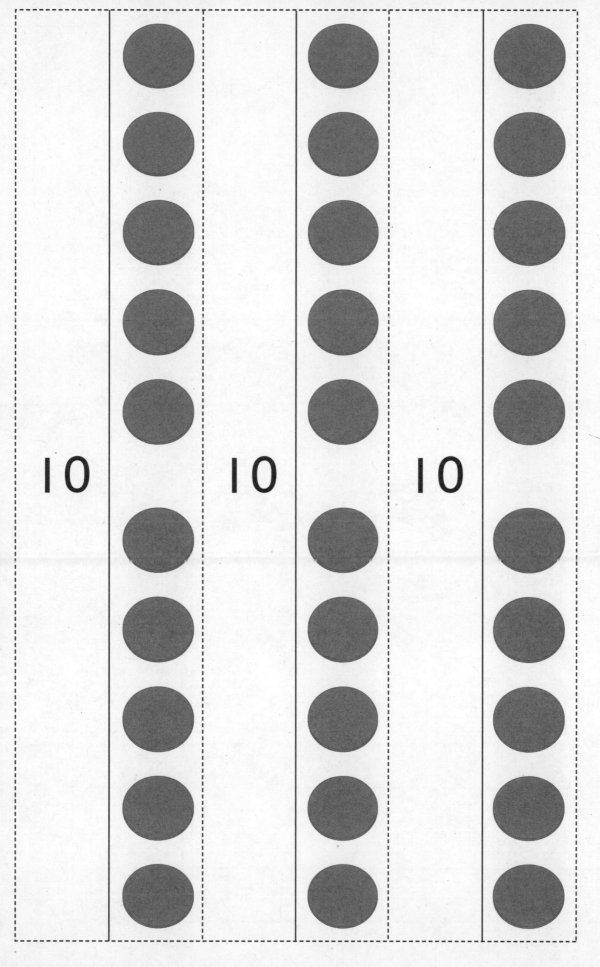

Cut on dashed lines. **Fold** on solid lines and tape at top and bottom.

© Houghton Mifflin Harcourt Publishing Company

10   10   10

10-Counter Strips

Connect the dots from 1 through 20 and color the Ten Bug.

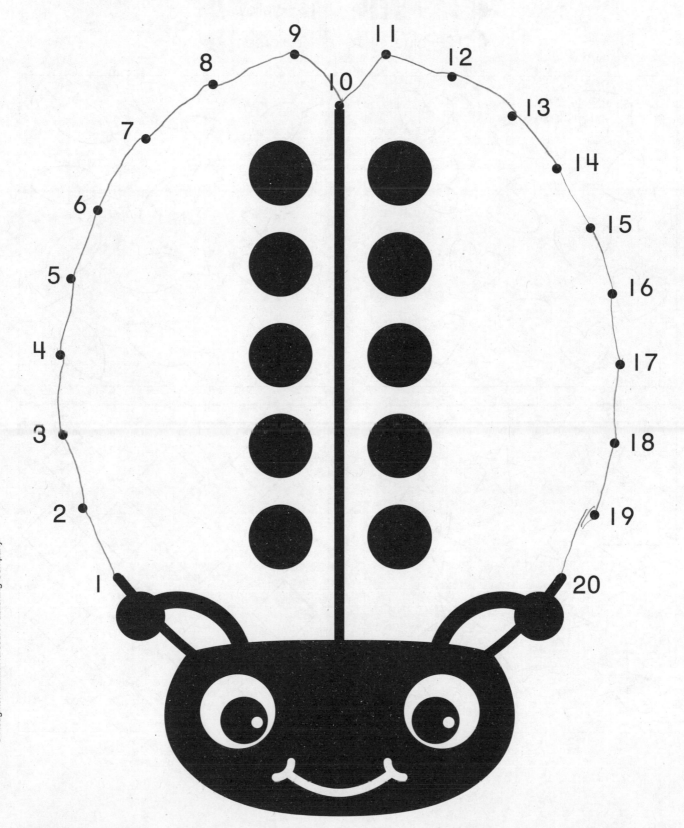

Ring a group of 10 in each box. Count and color the items. Use the colors shown.

11—red   13—yellow

12—blue   14—green

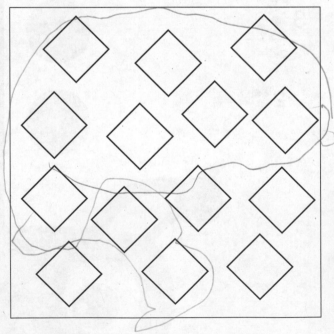

Family Letter

Content Overview

Dear Family:

Your child is learning about partners of numbers. We call the number pairs that make up a number "partners" because they go together to make that number. For example,

6 has partners: 1 and 5   2 and 4   3 and 3

6 = 1 + 5

6 = 2 + 4

6 = 3 + 3

The partner idea is very important for understanding numbers. It will help your child understand addition and subtraction. You can help your child see partners in everyday life. When you have a small number of objects, for example, 5 crackers, you can ask your child to make the partners of 5. Your child can show 1 and 4 crackers and can also show 2 and 3 crackers. Doing this often with different objects will help your child understand numbers.

Thank you!

Sincerely,
Your child's teacher

CA CC

Unit 3 addresses the following standards from the *Common Core State Standards for Mathematics with California Additions*: **K.CC.1, K.CC.2, K.CC.3, K.CC.4, K.CC.4a, K.CC.4b, K.CC.4c, K.CC.5, K.CC.6, K.CC.7, K.OA.1, K.OA.2, K.OA.3, K.OA.5, K.NBT.1, K.MD.3, K.G.1, K.G.2, K.G.4, K.G.6,** and all Mathematical Practices.

Estimada familia:

Su niño está aprendiendo sobre las partes de los números. Llamamos "partes" a los pares de números que pueden juntarse para formar un determinado número. Por ejemplo,

6 tiene las partes: 1 y 5   2 y 4   3 y 3

6 = 1 + 5

6 = 2 + 4

6 = 3 + 3

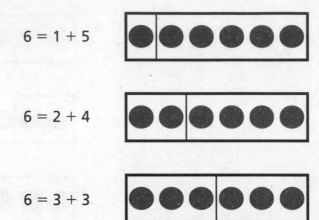

La idea de las partes es muy importante para entender los números. Ayudará a su niño a entender la suma y la resta. Ud. puede ayudar a su niño a ver partes en la vida diaria. Cuando tenga un pequeño número de objetos, por ejemplo 5 galletas, puede pedirle a su niño que muestre las partes de 5. Su niño puede mostrar 1 galleta y 4 galletas y también 2 galletas y 3 galletas. Hacer esto a menudo con distintos objetos puede ayudar a su niño a entender los números.

¡Gracias!

Atentamente,
El maestro de su niño

CA CC

En la Unidad 3 se aplican los siguientes estándares auxiliares, contenidos en los *Estándares Estatales Comunes de Matemáticas con Adiciones para California*: **K.CC.1, K.CC.2, K.CC.3, K.CC.4, K.CC.4a, K.CC.4b, K.CC.4c, K.CC.5, K.CC.6, K.CC.7, K.OA.1, K.OA.2, K.OA.3, K.OA.5, K.NBT.1, K.MD.3, K.G.1, K.G.2, K.G.4, K.G.6** y todos los de prácticas matemáticas.

Count how many. Write the number.

1.

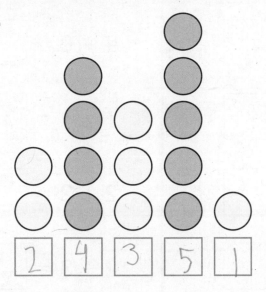

| 2 | 4 | 3 | 5 | 1 |

2.

5

1

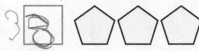

2

4

3 8

3.

1

1

2

5

3

4.

| 4 | 2 | 8 | 5 | 1 |

3

5. Write the numbers 1–10.

| 1 | 2 | 3 | 4 | 5 | 6 | 7 | 8 | 9 | 10 |

6. Add the numbers.

$0 + 3 = \boxed{3}$ $2 + 0 = \boxed{2}$ $4 + 0 = \boxed{4}$

$2 + 1 = \boxed{3}$ $1 + 4 = \boxed{5}$ $1 + 1 = \boxed{2}$

$0 + 2 = \boxed{2}$ $1 + 2 = \boxed{3}$ $2 + 2 = \boxed{4}$

$0 + 3 = \boxed{3}$ $3 + 1 = \boxed{4}$ $2 + 3 = \boxed{5}$

$4 + 1 = \boxed{5}$ $5 + 0 = \boxed{5}$ $1 + 4 = \boxed{5}$

7. Subtract the numbers.

$3 - 0 = \boxed{3}$ $2 - 0 = \boxed{2}$ $4 - 0 = \boxed{4}$

$4 - 1 = \boxed{3}$ $5 - 1 = \boxed{4}$ $1 - 1 = \boxed{0}$

$5 - 2 = \boxed{3}$ $4 - 2 = \boxed{2}$ $3 - 2 = \boxed{1}$

$3 - 3 = \boxed{0}$ $5 - 3 = \boxed{2}$ $4 - 3 = \boxed{1}$

$5 - 4 = \boxed{1}$ $4 - 4 = \boxed{0}$ $5 - 5 = \boxed{0}$

Addition and Subtraction Stories: Park Scene

Dear Family:

When children first start counting, they count objects one at a time. Helping children see 5-groups and 10-groups enables them to understand larger (greater) numbers. We are learning that if we can see groups of objects as 5-groups and 10-groups, then we can understand greater numbers. Children learn to make these groups with objects. Later, they will see them as organized groups in their minds.

Your child is learning that the teen numbers 11, 12, 13, 14, 15, 16, 17, 18, and 19 each have a 10 inside: $11 = 10 + 1$, $12 = 10 + 2$, and so on through $19 = 10 + 9$.

Have your child practice counting groups of objects. Your child can find and separate the 10-group from the total quantity to see the 10 hiding inside the teen number.

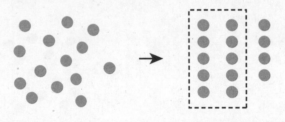

fourteen   is   ten and four

Your child can then show this number by using the number cards on the next page.

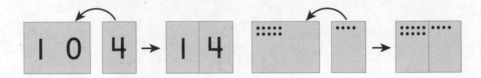

Thank you for your cooperation!

Sincerely,
Your child's teacher

 CA CC

Unit 3 addresses the following standards from the *Common Core State Standards for Mathematics with California Additions*: **K.CC.1, K.CC.2, K.CC.3, K.CC.4, K.CC.4a, K.CC.4b, K.CC.4c, K.CC.5, K.CC.6, K.CC.7, K.OA.1, K.OA.2, K.OA.3, K.OA.5, K.NBT.1, K.MD.3, K.G.1, K.G.2, K.G.4, K.G.6,** and all Mathematical Practices.

Carta a la familia

Un vistazo general al contenido

Estimada familia:

Cuando los niños empiezan a contar, suelen contar los objetos uno por uno. Ayudarlos a ver los objetos en grupos de 5 y grupos de 10, les facilita el aprendizaje de números más grandes (mayores). Estamos aprendiendo que si podemos ver grupos de objetos como grupos de 5 y grupos de 10, entonces podemos entender números más grandes. Los niños aprenden a formar estos grupos con objetos. Más adelante, los verán mentalmente como grupos organizados.

Su niño está aprendiendo que los números 11, 12, 13, 14, 15, 16, 17, 18 y 19 contienen 10: 11 = 10 + 1, 12 = 10 + 2, y así sucesivamente, hasta 19 = 10 + 9.

Pida a su niño que practique contando grupos de objetos. Su niño puede separar el grupo de 10 de la cantidad total, para ver el 10 escondido en los números de 11 a 19.

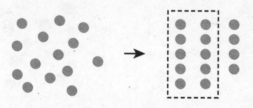

catorce   es   diez más cuatro

Después, su niño puede mostrar este número usando las tarjetas de números de la página siguiente.

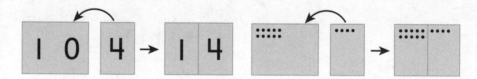

¡Gracias por su colaboración!

Atentamente,
El maestro de su niño

CA CC

En la Unidad 3 se aplican los siguientes estándares auxiliares, contenidos en los *Estándares Estatales Comunes de Matemáticas con Adiciones para California*: **K.CC.1, K.CC.2, K.CC.3, K.CC.4, K.CC.4a, K.CC.4b, K.CC.4c, K.CC.5, K.CC.6, K.CC.7, K.OA.1, K.OA.2, K.OA.3, K.OA.5, K.NBT.1, K.MD.3, K.G.1, K.G.2, K.G.4, K.G.6** y todos los de prácticas matemáticas.

1	2	3	4	5
6	7	8	9	1
0				

More Groups of 10

Name

CA CC Content Standards K.CC.2, K.CC.3, K.CC.4c,
K.CC.5, K.OA.5 Mathematical Practices MP.7, MP.8

VOCABULARY
5-group

1. Draw the circles on the Number Parade. Use a **5-group**.

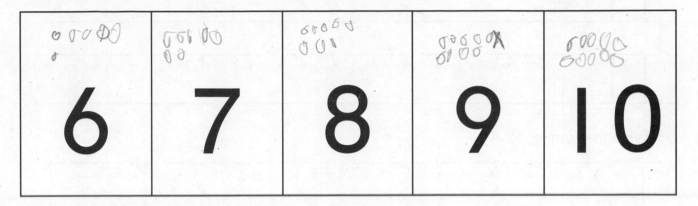

6   7   8   9   10

2. Use the 5-group. Draw to show the number.

9 =

6 =

8 =

10 =

7 =

3. Write the number.

9 =

5 =

4 =

6 =

2 =

8 =

7 =

8 =

7 =

6 =

7 =

3 =

4. Write the number 11.

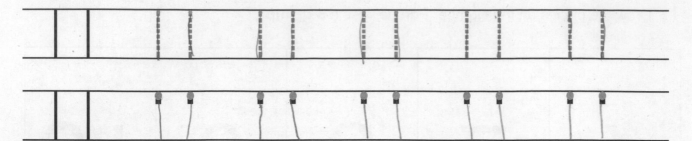

5. Write the number 12.

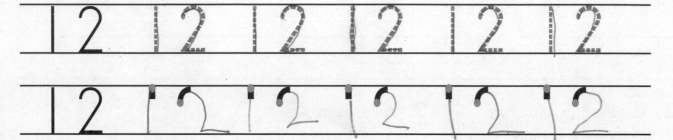

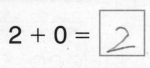
PATH to
FLUENCY

6. Add the numbers.

2 + 0 = **2**	0 + 3 = **3**	5 + 0 = **5**
1 + 1 = **2**	1 + 2 = **3**	4 + 1 = **5**
2 + 2 = **4**	3 + 2 = **5**	2 + 3 = **5**

7. Subtract the numbers.

4 − 0 = **4**	1 − 0 = **1**	5 − 0 = **5**
4 − 1 = **B**	2 − 1 = **1**	3 − 1 = **7**
4 − 2 = **2**	5 − 2 = **3**	5 − 3 = **2**

More Groups of 10

Family Letter

Content Overview

Dear Family:

When children first learn to write numbers, emphasis is placed on forming the numbers correctly. Children begin by tracing, and then are provided with starting points for their pencils. Learning the correct technique helps children learn to write numbers neatly and consistently.

After awhile, children no longer need these hints and are able to write without guide lines or starting points. It is easier for many children to write smaller figures, since they have greater control of the writing tool. With practice, children will gain confidence and speed in writing numbers.

In Unit 3, children continue to practice writing numbers, including 2-digit numbers from 11 to 20. They are already familiar with the individual numbers they will be using. When writing 2-digit numbers, children learn the proper placement and spacing between numbers. The numbers should not be too close together or too far apart, but just the right distance to be read and understood.

13	1 3	13

Please help and encourage your child as he or she learns to write numbers. This will take time and practice.

Thank you!

Sincerely,
Your child's teacher

 CA CC

Unit 3 addresses the following standards from the *Common Core State Standards for Mathematics with California Additions*: **K.CC.1, K.CC.2, K.CC.3, K.CC.4, K.CC.4a, K.CC.4b, K.CC.4c, K.CC.5, K.CC.6, K.CC.7, K.OA.1, K.OA.2, K.OA.3, K.OA.5, K.NBT.1, K.MD.3, K.G.1, K.G.2, K.G.4, K.G.6,** and all Mathematical Practices.

Estimada familia:

Cuando los niños aprenden a escribir los números, se enfatiza que deben trazarlos correctamente. Se comienza calcando y luego, se les proporcionan puntos desde donde deben comenzar con sus lápices. Aprender la técnica exacta les servirá a los niños para escribir consistentemente los números de manera correcta.

Después de un tiempo, ya no necesitan estas pistas y pueden escribir sin líneas que les guíen y sin puntos donde comenzar. Es más fácil para muchos niños trazar números pequeños, ya que así tienen más control del instrumento de escritura. Con práctica, los niños adquirirán confianza y velocidad para escribir los números.

En la Unidad 3, los niños continúan practicando la escritura de números, incluyendo los números de 2 dígitos del 11 al 20. Ya están familiarizados con los números individuales que estarán usando. Al escribir números de 2 dígitos, deben aprender su colocación correcta y la distancia correcta que debe haber entre los dígitos. No deben estar demasiado juntos ni demasiado separados, la distancia debe ser adecuada para poder leerlos y comprenderlos.

Por favor ayude a su niño a escribir los números. Esto requerirá tiempo y práctica. Anímelo y apóyelo durante el aprendizaje.

¡Gracias!

Atentamente,
El maestro de su niño

© Houghton Mifflin Harcourt Publishing Company

CA CC

En la Unidad 3 se aplican los siguientes estándares auxiliares, contenidos en los *Estándares Estatales Comunes de Matemáticas con Adiciones para California*: K.CC.1, K.CC.2, K.CC.3, K.CC.4, K.CC.4a, K.CC.4b, K.CC.4c, K.CC.5, K.CC.6, K.CC.7, K.OA.1, K.OA.2, K.OA.3, K.OA.5, K.NBT.1, K.MD.3, K.G.1, K.G.2, K.G.4, K.G.6 y todos los de prácticas matemáticas.

Name _____

CA CC Content Standards K.CC.3, K.OA.5
Mathematical Practices MP.6, MP.8

1. Write the number 13.

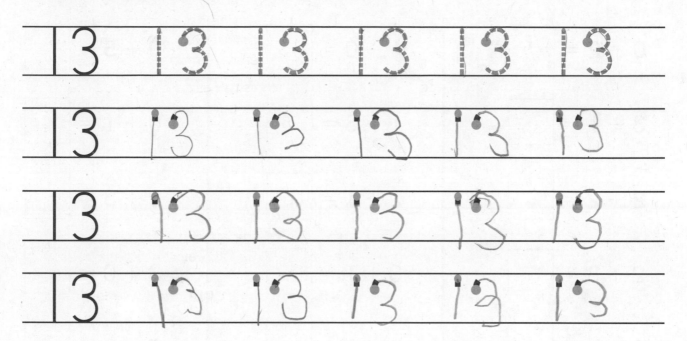

2. Write the number 14.

3. Add the numbers.

$0 + 2 = \boxed{2}$ $1 + 0 = \boxed{1}$ $0 + 5 = \boxed{5}$

$3 + 1 = \boxed{4}$ $1 + 3 = \boxed{4}$ $0 + 1 = \boxed{1}$

$2 + 2 = \boxed{4}$ $2 + 1 = \boxed{3}$ $2 + 3 = \boxed{5}$

$2 + 3 = \boxed{5}$ $3 + 1 = \boxed{4}$ $3 + 0 = \boxed{3}$

$0 + 4 = \boxed{4}$ $4 + 1 = \boxed{5}$ $5 + 0 = \boxed{5}$

4. Subtract the numbers.

$1 - 0 = \boxed{1}$ $4 - 0 = \boxed{4}$ $2 - 0 = \boxed{2}$

$5 - 1 = \boxed{4}$ $3 - 1 = \boxed{2}$ $4 - 1 = \boxed{3}$

$3 - 2 = \boxed{1}$ $2 - 2 = \boxed{0}$ $4 - 2 = \boxed{2}$

$5 - 3 = \boxed{2}$ $4 - 3 = \boxed{1}$ $3 - 3 = \boxed{0}$

$4 - 4 = \boxed{0}$ $5 - 5 = \boxed{0}$ $5 - 4 = \boxed{1}$

Model Partners Through 6 with Counters

VOCABULARY
5-group

1. Draw the circles on the Number Parade. Use a **5-group**.

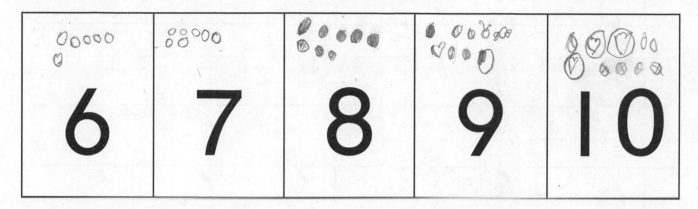

| 6 | 7 | 8 | 9 | 10 |

2. Use the 5-group. Draw to show the number.

6 = ⬜
7 = ⬜
8 = ⬜
9 = ⬜
10 = ⬜

3. Write the number.

3 = ⬜
9 = ⬜
2 = ⬜
8 = ⬜
6 = ⬜
10 = ⬜

7 = ⬜
6 = ⬜
7 = ⬜
4 = ⬜
9 = ⬜
5 = ⬜

4. Write the number 15.

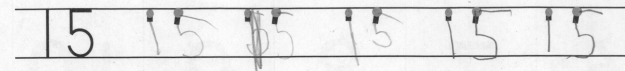

5. Write the number 16.

PATH to FLUENCY

6. Add the numbers.

5 + 0 = 5	0 + 3 = 3	4 + 0 = 4
2 + 1 = 3	1 + 2 = 3	1 + 1 = 2
2 + 2 = 4	3 + 2 = 5	1 + 4 = 5

7. Subtract the numbers.

3 − 0 = 3	1 − 0 = 1	2 − 0 = 2
2 − 1 = 1	5 − 1 = 4	3 − 1 = 2
5 − 2 = 3	5 − 4 = 1	4 − 2 = 2

More Addition and Subtraction Stories: Park Scene

CA CC Content Standards **K.G.2, K.G.6**
Mathematical Practices **MP.3, MP.6, MP.7, MP.8**

Build the shape.

1.

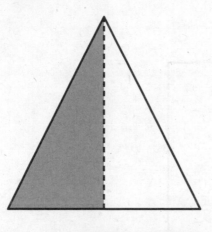

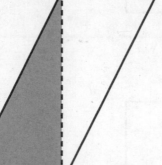

2.

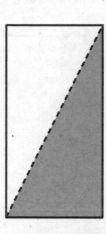

3.

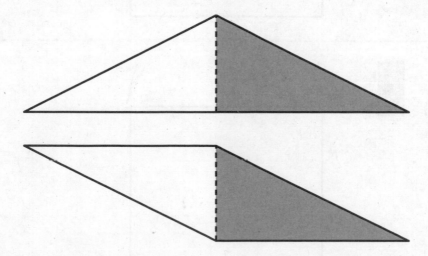

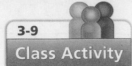

Name _____

Build. Trace the shapes. Color.

4. Use 4 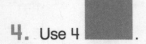.

5. Use 4 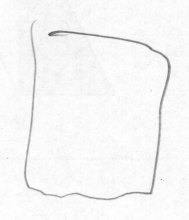.

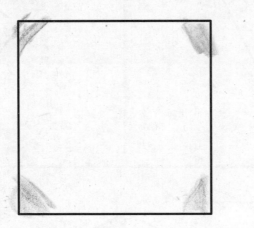

6. Use 1 ▢ and 1 ▮.

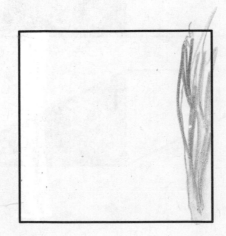
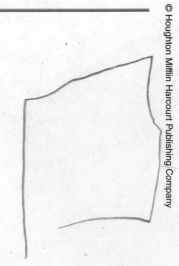

Build. Trace the shapes. Color.

1.

2.

3.
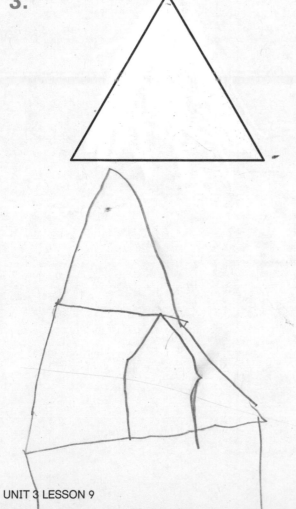

4.
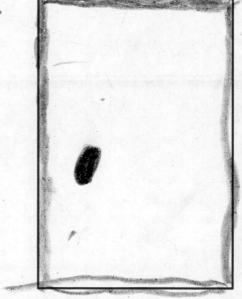

Name _____

Build. Trace the shapes. Color.

5.
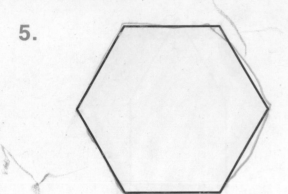

6.
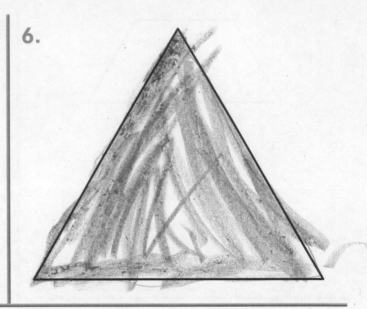

Build a shape. Trace the outline of the shape.

7.
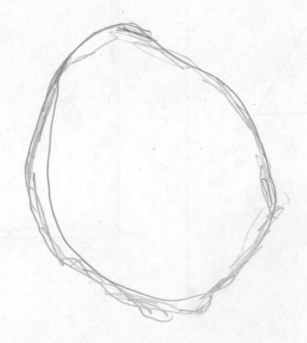

Make New Shapes

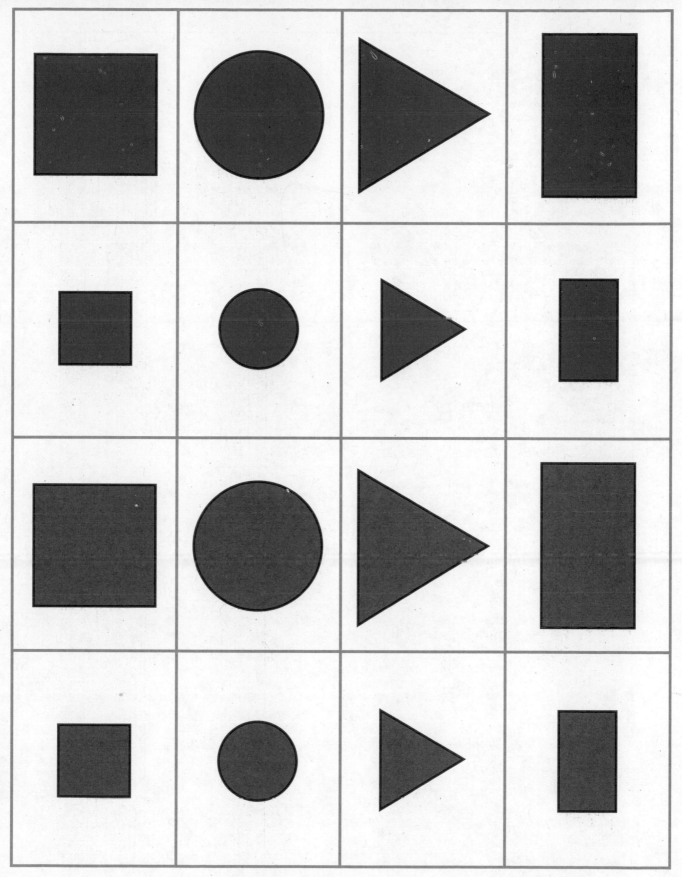

Sorting Cards

Sorting Cards

Name

CA CC Content Standards K.CC.2, K.CC.3, K.CC.4b, K.CC.4c, K.CC.5 Mathematical Practices MP.3, MP.6, MP.7

1. Draw circles for 1–10. Show the **5-groups**.

1	
2	
3	
4	
5	
6	
7	
8	○○○○○ ○○○
9	
10	

2. Use the 5-group. Draw to show the number.

9 = ○○○○○

7 = ○○○○○

8 = ○○○○○

10 = ○○○○○

6 = ○○○○○

9 = ○○○○○

7 = ○○○○○

8 = ○○○○○

3. Count how many. Write the number.

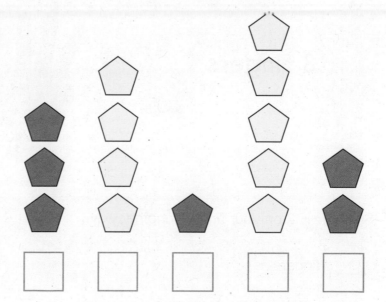

☐ ☐ ☐ ☐ ☐

Name _____

Help Puzzled Penguin.

4. Look at Puzzled Penguin's answers.

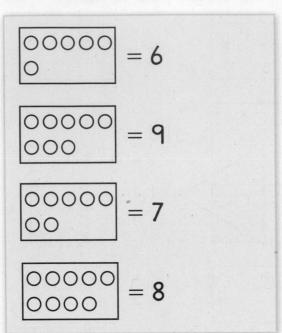

Am I correct?

---

5. Look at what Puzzled Penguin wrote.

8 fingers

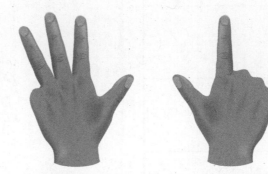

Show 4 + 2 on your fingers another way.

_____ fingers

Practice Addition and Subtraction Stories: Park Scene

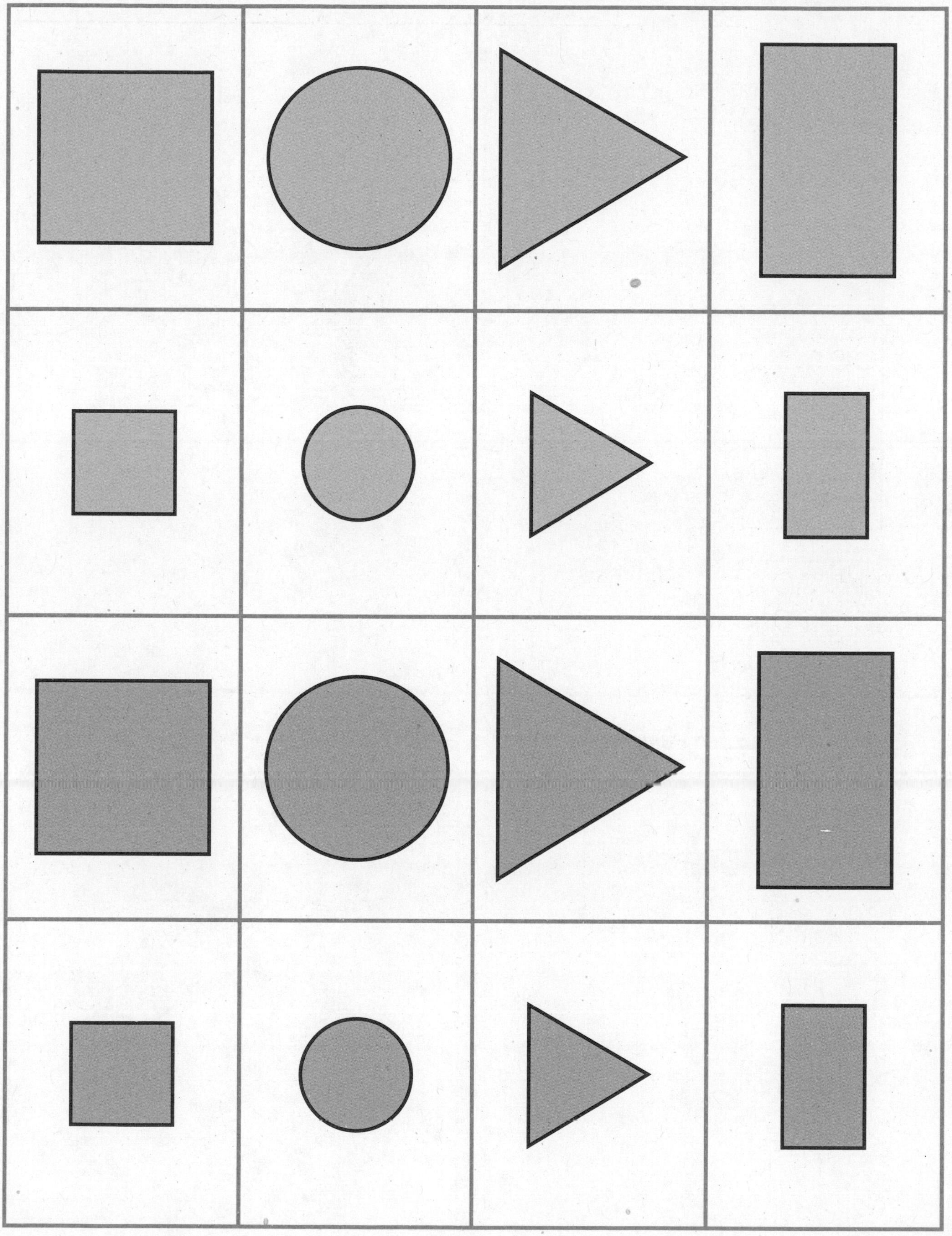

Sorting Cards

Sorting Cards

Name _____

CA CC Content Standards K.CC.2, K.CC.3, K.CC.4c, K.CC.5, K.CC.7, K.OA.5 Mathematical Practices MP.2

VOCABULARY
equal sign (=)
is not equal to sign (≠)

1. Draw circles for 1–10. Show the 5-group.

1	2	3	4	5	6	7	8	9	10
								○○○○○ ○○○○	

2. Write each number and an **equal sign (=)** or an **is not equal to sign (≠)**.

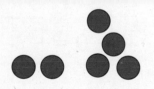

`2` ≠ `4`

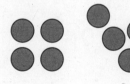

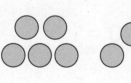

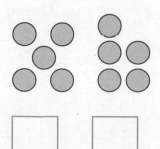

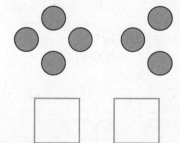

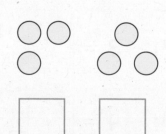

3. Add the numbers.

$0 + 4 =$ ☐ $0 + 0 =$ ☐ $1 + 0 =$ ☐

$3 + 1 =$ ☐ $1 + 2 =$ ☐ $4 + 1 =$ ☐

$2 + 2 =$ ☐ $2 + 0 =$ ☐ $0 + 2 =$ ☐

$2 + 3 =$ ☐ $3 + 1 =$ ☐ $3 + 2 =$ ☐

$4 + 0 =$ ☐ $1 + 4 =$ ☐ $0 + 5 =$ ☐

4. Subtract the numbers.

$0 - 0 =$ ☐ $1 - 0 =$ ☐ $4 - 0 =$ ☐

$3 - 1 =$ ☐ $4 - 1 =$ ☐ $2 - 1 =$ ☐

$5 - 2 =$ ☐ $3 - 2 =$ ☐ $2 - 2 =$ ☐

$4 - 3 =$ ☐ $5 - 3 =$ ☐ $3 - 3 =$ ☐

$4 - 4 =$ ☐ $5 - 2 =$ ☐ $5 - 1 =$ ☐

Practice Classifying

1. Write the number. Draw it using the 5-group.

= ☐

⬚ (5-group box with 5 circles)

= ☐

⬚ (5-group box with 5 circles)

= ☐

⬚ (5-group box with 5 circles)

= ☐

⬚ (5-group box with 5 circles)

2. Use the 5-group. Draw to show the number.

7 = ⬚ (box with 4 circles)   10 = ⬚ (box with 5 circles)

9 = ⬚ (box with 5 circles)   7 = ⬚ (box with 5 circles)

6 = ⬚ (box with 5 circles)   6 = ⬚ (box with 5 circles)

8 = ⬚ (box with 5 circles)   9 = ⬚ (box with 5 circles)

3. Write the number.

⬚ (5 circles top, 1 circle bottom) = ☐   ⬚ (5 circles top, 2 circles bottom) = ☐

⬚ (5 circles top, 2 circles bottom) = ☐   ⬚ (5 circles top, 3 circles bottom) = ☐

⬚ (4 circles) = ☐   ⬚ (5 circles) = ☐

⬚ (5 circles top, 3 circles bottom) = ☐   ⬚ (5 circles top, 4 circles bottom) = ☐

4. Draw a ring around every 5-group.

Write the numbers shown by the circles.

5. Look at what Puzzled Penguin drew.

Help Puzzled Penguin.

1	2	3	4	5	6	7	8	9	10

Am I correct?

Build Teen Numbers

Name

CA CC Content Standards K.CC.3, K.CC.4c, K.CC.5, K.CC.7, K.OA.5 Mathematical Practices MP.2, MP.6, MP.8

1. Draw circles for 1–10. Show the 5-group.

1	2	3	4	5	6	7	8	9	10
							○○○○○ ○○○		

2. Write each number and an **equal sign (=)** or an **is not equal to sign (≠)**.

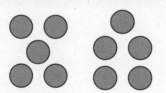 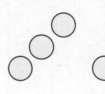 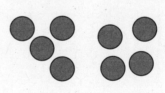

5 = 5 □ □ □ □

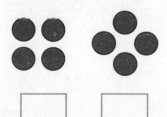 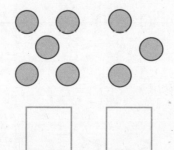 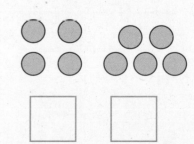

□ □ □ □ □ □

3. Write the number 15.

15 15 15 15 15 15

15

4. Write the number 16.

16 16 16 16 16 16

16

PATH to FLUENCY

5. Add the numbers.

$0 + 2 = \boxed{}$ $0 + 0 = \boxed{}$ $3 + 0 = \boxed{}$

$1 + 3 = \boxed{}$ $1 + 2 = \boxed{}$ $4 + 1 = \boxed{}$

$2 + 3 = \boxed{}$ $3 + 2 = \boxed{}$ $0 + 4 = \boxed{}$

6. Subtract the numbers.

$4 - 0 = \boxed{}$ $0 - 0 = \boxed{}$ $1 - 0 = \boxed{}$

$4 - 1 = \boxed{}$ $5 - 1 = \boxed{}$ $1 - 1 = \boxed{}$

$5 - 2 = \boxed{}$ $5 - 4 = \boxed{}$ $4 - 2 = \boxed{}$

Practice with 5-Groups

15

14

13

12

11

10 + 5

10 + 4

10 + 3

10 + 2

10 + 1

19

18

17

16

10 + 9

10 + 8

10 + 7

10 + 6

Teen Total Cards **133**

Name _____

CA CC Content Standards K.OA.1, K.OA.3
Mathematical Practices MP.7

Write the **partners**.

2

☐ + ☐

3

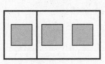

☐ + ☐

3

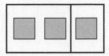

☐ + ☐

4

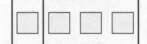

☐ + ☐

4

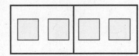

☐ + ☐

4

☐ + ☐

5

☐ + ☐

5

☐ + ☐

5

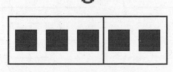

☐ + ☐

5

☐ + ☐

Write the partners.

6

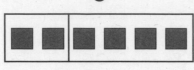

$\square + \square$

6

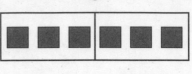

$\square + \square$

6

$\square + \square$

6

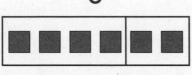

$\square + \square$

6

$\square + \square$

7

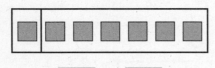

$\square + \square$

7

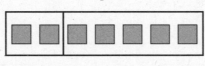

$\square + \square$

7

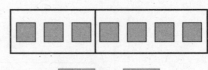

$\square + \square$

7

$\square + \square$

7

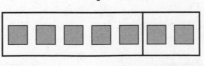

$\square + \square$

7

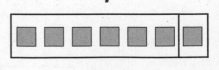

$\square + \square$

Practice with Partners

Dear Family:

In the next few days, please find 20 of the same kind of small object that your child can take to school and paste onto a sheet of paper. For example, your child can use buttons or stickers, or you can cut out 20 small pieces of paper or fabric.

The objects will be used for an activity to help your child learn to see the group of 10 inside each of the teen numbers: 11, 12, 13, 14, 15, 16, 17, 18, and 19.

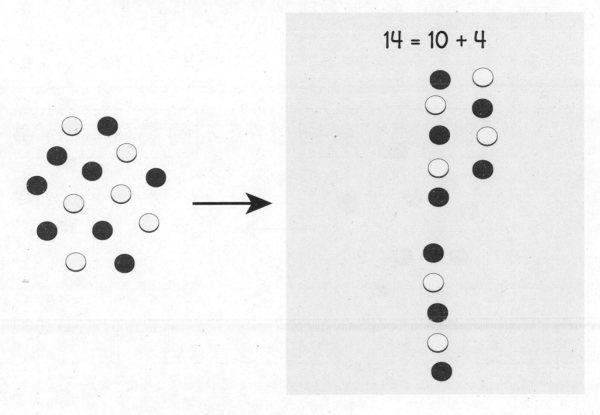

Thank you for your cooperation!

Sincerely,
Your child's teacher

CA CC

Unit 3 addresses the following standards from the *Common Core State Standards for Mathematics with California Additions*: **K.CC.1, K.CC.2, K.CC.3, K.CC.4, K.CC.4a, K.CC.4b, K.CC.4c, K.CC.5, K.CC.6, K.CC.7, K.OA.1, K.OA.2, K.OA.3, K.OA.5, K.NBT.1, K.MD.3, K.G.1, K.G.2, K.G.4, K.G.6,** and all Mathematical Practices.

Estimada familia:

Durante los días siguientes, por favor busque 20 objetos pequeños, del mismo tipo, que su niño pueda llevar a la escuela y pegar en una hoja de papel. Por ejemplo, su niño puede usar botones o adhesivos, o usted puede cortar 20 pedacitos de papel o tela.

Los objetos se usarán en una actividad que ayudará a su niño a identificar el grupo de 10 que hay en cada uno de los números de 11 a 19: 11, 12, 13, 14, 15, 16, 17, 18 y 19.

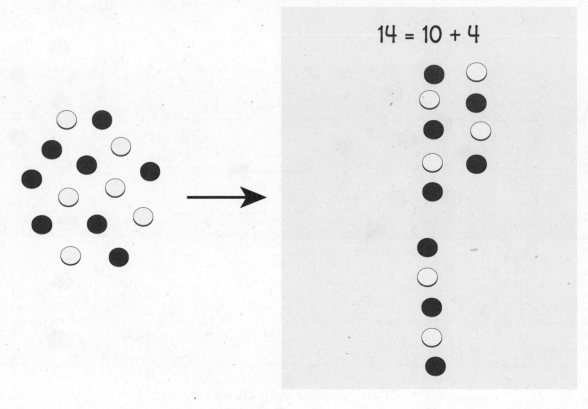

¡Gracias por su colaboración!

Atentamente,
El maestro de su niño

CA CC

En la Unidad 3 se aplican los siguientes estándares auxiliares, contenidos en los *Estándares Estatales Comunes de Matemáticas con Adiciones para California*: **K.CC.1, K.CC.2, K.CC.3, K.CC.4, K.CC.4a, K.CC.4b, K.CC.4c, K.CC.5, K.CC.6, K.CC.7, K.OA.1, K.OA.2, K.OA.3, K.OA.5, K.NBT.1, K.MD.3, K.G.1, K.G.2, K.G.4, K.G.6** y todos los de prácticas matemáticas.

I. Write the **partners**. Look for **switched partners**.

5

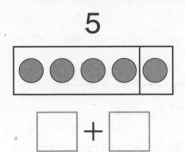

☐ + ☐

5

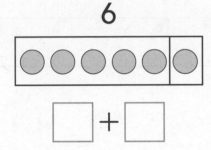

☐ + ☐

5

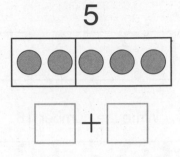

☐ + ☐

6

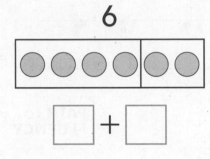

☐ + ☐

6

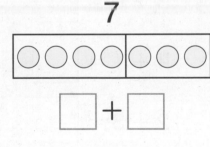

☐ + ☐

6

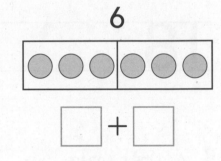

☐ + ☐

7

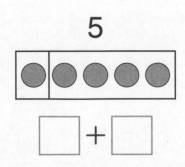

☐ + ☐

7

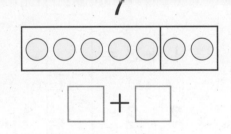

☐ + ☐

7

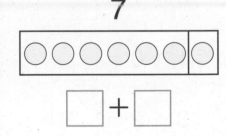

☐ + ☐

5

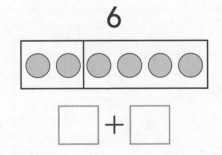

☐ + ☐

6

☐ + ☐

7

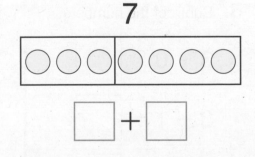

☐ + ☐

2. Write the number 17.

17   17   17   17   17   17

17

3. Write the number 18.

18   18   18   18   18   18

18

PATH to FLUENCY

4. Add the numbers.

0 + 1 = ☐   0 + 4 = ☐   3 + 0 = ☐

1 + 0 = ☐   1 + 3 = ☐   4 + 1 = ☐

3 + 2 = ☐   2 + 2 = ☐   2 + 3 = ☐

5. Subtract the numbers.

3 − 0 = ☐   2 − 0 = ☐   5 − 0 = ☐

3 − 1 = ☐   5 − 1 = ☐   2 − 1 = ☐

5 − 2 = ☐   5 − 3 = ☐   4 − 3 = ☐

Build Teen Numbers with Classroom Objects

1. Puzzled Penguin showed the partners
for two teen numbers and wrote the total.
Help Puzzled Penguin.

Am I correct?

$\underline{12} = 10 + 3 \quad \underline{13} = 10 + 2$

2. Draw the buttons. Write the total.

$\underline{} = 10 + 5 \quad \underline{} = 10 + 1$

3. Write the number 19.

19 19 19 19 19

19

4. Write the number 20.

20 20 20 20 20

20

PATH to
FLUENCY

5. Add the numbers.

$2 + 0 =$ ☐ $0 + 2 =$ ☐ $4 + 0 =$ ☐

$1 + 2 =$ ☐ $0 + 1 =$ ☐ $3 + 1 =$ ☐

$1 + 4 =$ ☐ $5 + 0 =$ ☐ $2 + 3 =$ ☐

6. Subtract the numbers.

$1 - 0 =$ ☐ $4 - 0 =$ ☐ $2 - 0 =$ ☐

$4 - 1 =$ ☐ $1 - 1 =$ ☐ $2 - 1 =$ ☐

$4 - 2 =$ ☐ $5 - 2 =$ ☐ $3 - 2 =$ ☐

Show Teen Numbers with Classroom Objects

Name _____

CA CC Content Standards **K.CC.5, K.G.1, K.G.2**
Mathematical Practices **MP.2, MP.3, MP.6, MP.7**

Color all the shapes of one kind the same color.

Count the number of each shape in the picture. Write the number.

Draw your own smiling faces!

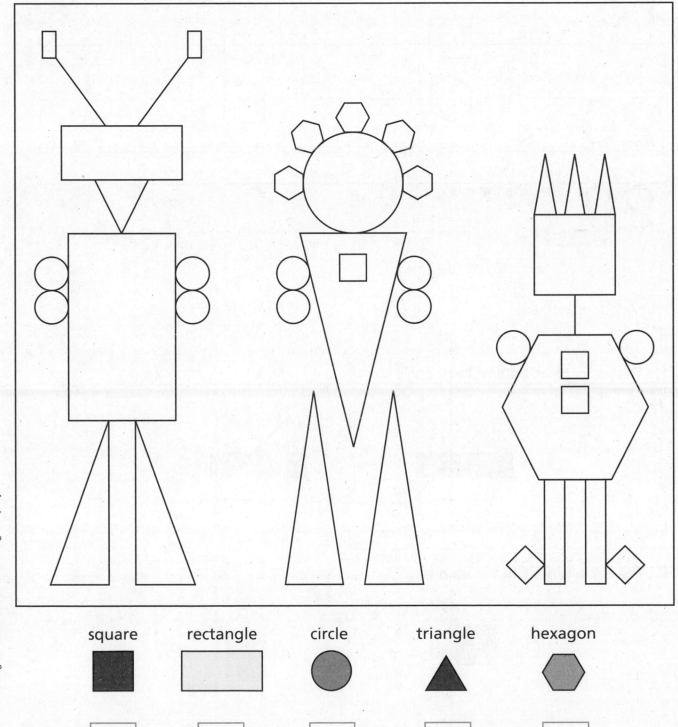

square	rectangle	circle	triangle	hexagon
▢	▭	●	▲	⬡
☐	☐	☐	☐	☐

Name _____

Circle the picture that matches the statement.

1. The hexagon is **below** the square.

2. The circle is **beside** the triangle.

3. The rectangle is **behind** the triangle.

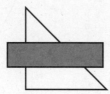 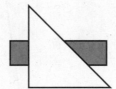

4. The circle is **next to** the square.

Focus on Mathematical Practices

Write the partners.

1.

6

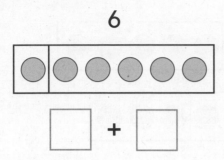

☐ + ☐

2.

6

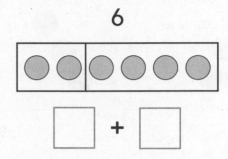

☐ + ☐

3. Ring a group of 10. Count all of the stars.
Write how many in all.

4. Ring the number. Draw it using the 5-group.

6
7
8

5. Write each number. Ring = or ≠.

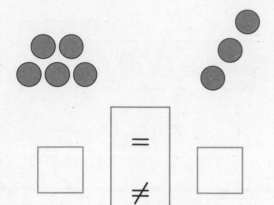

	=	
	≠	

6. Choose all the partners that are equal to 6.

○

○

○

---

7. Add the numbers. Ring the answer.

$3 + 1 = \boxed{}$

2	3	4

---

8. Subtract the numbers. Ring the answer.

$4 - 2 = \boxed{}$

2	3	4

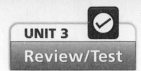
Use the picture below to complete Exercises 9–12.

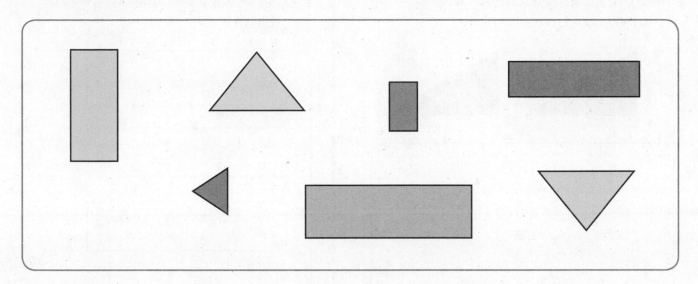

9. Ring all of the four-sided shapes.

10. How many triangles are there?

○ 2   ○ 3   ○ 4

11. How many rectangles are there?

○ 2   ○ 3   ○ 4

12. Are there more triangles or rectangles? Ring the shape.

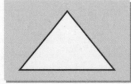   

13. Two triangles are joined. Draw a shape they could make.

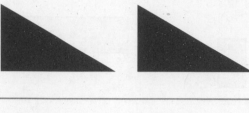

14. Draw a triangle. Draw a circle below it.

15. Draw to show the story problem. Write the answer.

Shane sees 5 butterflies. Tony sees 2 butterflies.

How many butterflies do they see in all?

California Common Core Standards for Mathematical Content

K.CC Counting and Cardinality

Know number names and the count sequence.

K.CC.1	Count to 100 by ones and by tens.	Unit 1 Lesson 17; Unit 2 Lessons 1, 2, 6, 7, 8, 10, 12, 16, 18, 19; Unit 3 Lessons 1, 2, 3; Unit 4 Lessons 12, 15, 16, 17; Unit 5 Lessons 2, 3, 5, 8, 13 **Daily Routine:** Counting Tens and Ones Routine **Quick Practice:** Oral Counting 1–10, Show Fingers 1–10, Giant Number Cards 1–5, Count by Ones from 20 Through 60
K.CC.2	Count forward beginning from a given number within the known sequence (instead of having to begin at 1).	Unit 1 Lesson 7; Unit 2 Lessons 9, 12, 15, 16, 18, 19; Unit 3 Lessons 5, 7, 11; Unit 4 Lesson 15; Unit 5 Lessons 10, 13 **Daily Routine:** Counting Tens and Ones Routine **Quick Practice:** Saying and Showing the 5-Group Pattern, Seeing and Hearing the 5-Group Pattern, The 5-Group Pattern for 6–10, Connect the 5-Group Pattern to Fingers, Count from 10 Through 20 Using Finger Freeze, Say Numbers 11 Through 20 in Order, Count by Ones from 20 Through 60
K.CC.3	Write numbers from 0 to 20. Represent a number of objects with a written numeral 0–20 (with 0 representing a count of no objects).	Unit 1 Lessons 12, 13, 14, 16, 17; Unit 2 Lessons 1, 2, 5, 7, 8, 9, 10, 11, 12, 14, 15, 16, 18, 19; Unit 3 Lessons 1, 4, 5, 6, 7, 11, 12, 13, 14, 18, 19; Unit 4 Lessons 3, 8, 10, 13 16, 18, 20; Unit 5 Lessons 2, 4, 5, 7, 8, 10, 11, 14, 16, 17, 20, 23 **Daily Routine:** Counting Tens and Ones Routine **Quick Practice:** Giant Number Cards 1–5, Giant Number Cards 6–10

Count to tell the number of objects.

K.CC.4a	Understand the relationship between numbers and quantities; connect counting to cardinality. **a.** When counting objects, say the number names in the standard order, pairing each object with one and only one number name and each number name with one and only one object.	Unit 1 Lessons 1, 2, 3, 4, 5, 6, 7, 8, 9, 11, 12, 13, 14, 15, 16, 17; Unit 2 Lessons 3, 5, 8, 10, 11, 15, 18; Unit 3 Lesson 2; Unit 4 Lessons 1, 3, 12, 16, 20; Unit 5 Lesson 2 **Daily Routine:** Counting Tens and Ones Routine **Quick Practice:** Oral Counting 1–10, Show Fingers 1–10, Giant Number Cards 1–5, Giant Number Cards 6–10

K.CC.4b	Understand the relationship between numbers and quantities; connect counting to cardinality. **b.** Understand that the last number name said tells the number of objects counted. The number of objects is the same regardless of their arrangement or the order in which they were counted.	Unit 1 Lessons 1, 2, 3, 4, 5, 6, 7, 8, 9, 11, 12, 13, 14, 15, 16, 17; Unit 2 Lessons 3, 5, 8, 10, 11, 15; Unit 3 Lessons 2, 11, 15, 18, 19, 20; Unit 4 Lessons 1, 3, 12, 20 **Daily Routine:** Counting Tens and Ones Routine **Quick Practice:** Show Fingers 1–10, Giant Number Cards 1–5, Giant Number Cards 6–10
K.CC.4c	Understand the relationship between numbers and quantities; connect counting to cardinality. **c.** Understand that each successive number name refers to a quantity that is one larger.	Unit 2 Lessons 12, 14, 16, 19; Unit 3 Lessons 5, 7, 11, 12, 13, 14, 20; Unit 4 Lessons 3, 5, 7, 12, 15; Unit 5 Lessons 7, 9, 15, 19, 23 **Daily Routine:** Counting Tens and Ones Routine **Quick Practice:** Oral Counting 1–10, Show Fingers 1–10, Giant Number Cards 1–5, Creative Movement and Sounds
K.CC.5	Count to answer "how many?" questions about as many as 20 things arranged in a line, a rectangular array, or a circle, or as many as 10 things in a scattered configuration; given a number from 1–20, count out that many objects.	Unit 1 Lessons 13, 15, 16; Unit 2 Lessons 1, 2, 3, 4, 5, 7, 8, 9, 10, 12, 14, 15, 16, 18, 20; Unit 3 Lessons 1, 2, 5, 7, 8, 10, 11, 12, 13, 14, 15, 18, 19, 20, 21; Unit 4 Lessons 1, 5, 6, 7, 8, 16; Unit 5 Lessons 1, 2, 3, 4, 7, 14, 15, 16, 17, 19, 20 **Daily Routine:** Counting Tens and Ones Routine **Quick Practice:** Giant Number Cards 1–5, Giant Number Cards 6–10

Compare numbers.

K.CC.6	Identify whether the number of objects in one group is greater than, less than, or equal to the number of objects in another group, e.g., by using matching and counting strategies.	Unit 1 Lessons 9, 11, 12, 13, 15, 16, 17; Unit 2 Lesson 9; Unit 3 Lessons 10, 12; Unit 4 Lessons 6, 10, 20; Unit 5 Lessons 10, 16, 17, 20 **Daily Routine:** Counting Tens and Ones Routine
K.CC.7	Compare two numbers between 1 and 10 presented as written numerals.	Unit 3 Lessons 12, 14; Unit 5 Lessons 10, 16, 17, 20 **Daily Routine:** Counting Tens and Ones Routine

K.OA Operations and Algebraic Thinking

Understand addition as putting together and adding to, and understand subtraction as taking apart and taking from.

K.OA.1	Represent addition and subtraction with objects, fingers, mental images, drawings, sounds (e.g., claps), acting out situations, verbal explanations, expressions, or equations.	Unit 1 Lessons 6, 7, 8, 21; Unit 2 Lessons 2, 3, 5, 6, 7, 9, 10, 11, 12, 14, 15, 16, 19; Unit 3 Lessons 3, 4, 6, 7, 11, 15, 16, 17, 18, 19, 20; Unit 4 Lessons 1, 2, 3, 4, 5, 6, 7, 10, 12, 13, 15, 17, 18, 19, 20; Unit 5 Lessons 3, 4, 6, 7, 8, 10, 12, 13, 14, 15, 16, 18, 19 **Quick Practice:** Practice + 1, Practice + 1 Orally
K.OA.2	Solve addition and subtraction word problems, and add and subtract within 10, e.g., by using objects or drawings to represent the problem.	Unit 1 Lesson 14; Unit 2 Lessons 1, 2, 4, 6, 9, 10, 11, 12, 14, 15, 16, 19; Unit 3 Lessons 1, 3, 4, 7, 11, 16; Unit 4 Lessons 2, 4, 5, 6, 7, 10, 12, 15, 16, 18, 19, 20; Unit 5 Lessons 1, 3, 4, 6, 7, 10, 12, 13, 15, 16, 18, 19
K.OA.3	Decompose numbers less than or equal to 10 into pairs in more than one way, e.g., by using objects or drawings, and record each decomposition by a drawing or equation (e.g., 5 = 2 + 3 and 5 = 4 + 1).	Unit 2 Lessons 2, 5, 10, 12, 14, 16, 19, 20; Unit 3 Lessons 3, 4, 6, 16, 17, 18; Unit 4 Lessons 2, 4, 5, 7, 8, 11, 13, 18, 19; Unit 5 Lessons 3, 4, 5, 6, 7, 8, 9, 10, 11, 12, 13, 14, 15, 18
K.OA.4	For any number from 1 to 9, find the number that makes 10 when added to the given number, e.g. by using objects or drawings, and record the answer with a drawing or equation.	Unit 2 Lessons 10, 12, 14, 16, 19; Unit 4 Lessons 2, 4, 8, 11, 13, 18, 19; Unit 5 Lessons 2, 3, 4, 6, 8, 9, 11, 12, 13, 18 **Quick Practice:** The Partner Peek on the 10-Partner Showcase
K.OA.5	Fluently add and subtract within 5.	Unit 2 Lessons 4, 6, 9, 10, 15; Unit 3 Lessons 4, 5, 6, 7, 12, 14, 18, 19; Unit 4 Lessons 3, 12, 15, 16, 17, 18, 20; Unit 5 Lessons 1, 7, 10, 12, 13, 15, 18, 19

K.NBT Number and Operations in Base Ten

Work with numbers 11–19 to gain foundations for place value.

K.NBT.1	Compose and decompose numbers from 11 to 19 into ten ones and some further ones, e.g., by using objects or drawings, and record each composition or decomposition by a drawing or equation (e.g., 18 = 10 + 8); understand that these numbers are composed of ten ones and one, two, three, four, five, six, seven, eight, or nine ones.	Unit 3 Lessons 2, 3, 5, 6, 8, 13, 15, 17, 18, 19, 20; Unit 4 Lessons 3, 5, 7, 12, 16, 18, 20; Unit 5 Lessons 1, 3, 4, 5, 6, 7, 9, 10, 15, 17, 18, 19, 20, 23 **Quick Practice:** 10 and 1 Make 11…, Show, Say, and See 11–19

K.MD Measurement and Data

Describe and compare measurable attributes.

K.MD.1	Describe measurable attributes of objects, such as length or weight. Describe several measurable attributes of a single object.	Unit 5 Lessons 21, 22, 23
K.MD.2	Directly compare two objects with a measurable attribute in common, to see which object has "more of"/"less of" the attribute, and describe the difference.	Unit 5 Lessons 21, 22, 23

Classify objects and count the number of objects in each category.

K.MD.3	Classify objects into given categories; count the numbers of objects in each category and sort the categories by count.	Unit 1 Lesson 10; Unit 2 Lessons 13, 17, 20; Unit 3 Lessons 10, 12, 21; Unit 4 Lessons 1, 9, 22

K.G Geometry

Identify and describe shapes (squares, circles, triangles, rectangles, hexagons, cubes, cones, cylinders, and spheres).

K.G.1	Describe objects in the environment using names of shapes, and describe the relative positions of these objects using terms such as *above, below, beside, in front of, behind,* and *next to.*	Unit 1 Lessons 8, 10, 18; Unit 2 Lessons 13, 17, 20: Unit 3 Lessons 10, 12, 21; Unit 4 Lessons 9, 14, 21, 22
K.G.2	Correctly name shapes regardless of their orientations or overall size.	Unit 1 Lessons 8, 10, 18; Unit 2 Lessons 13, 17, 20: Unit 3 Lessons 9, 10, 12, 21; Unit 4 Lessons 9, 14, 21, 22
K.G.3	Identify shapes as two-dimensional (lying in a plane, "flat") or three-dimensional ("solid").	Unit 1 Lessons 8, 10, 18; Unit 4 Lessons 9, 14, 21

Analyze, compare, create, and compose shapes.

K.G.4	Analyze and compare two- and three-dimensional shapes, in different sizes and orientations, using informal language to describe their similarities, differences, parts (e.g., number of sides and vertices/"corners") and other attributes (e.g., having sides of equal length).	Unit 1 Lessons 8, 18; Unit 2 Lessons 13, 17; Unit 3 Lesson 21; Unit 4 Lessons 9, 14, 21, 22
K.G.5	Model shapes in the world by building shapes from components (e.g., sticks and clay balls) and drawing shapes.	Unit 1 Lessons 8, 10, 18; Unit 4 Lessons 9, 21
K.G.6	Compose simple shapes to form larger shapes.	Unit 3 Lesson 9; Unit 4 Lesson 21

California Common Core Standards for Mathematical Practice

MP.1 Make sense of problems and persevere in solving them.

Mathematically proficient students start by explaining to themselves the meaning of a problem and looking for entry points to its solution. They analyze givens, constraints, relationships, and goals. They make conjectures about the form and meaning of the solution and plan a solution pathway rather than simply jumping into a solution attempt. They consider analogous problems, and try special cases and simpler forms of the original problem in order to gain insight into its solution. They monitor and evaluate their progress and change course if necessary. Older students might, depending on the context of the problem, transform algebraic expressions or change the viewing window on their graphing calculator to get the information they need. Mathematically proficient students can explain correspondences between equations, verbal descriptions, tables, and graphs or draw diagrams of important features and relationships, graph data, and search for regularity or trends. Younger students might rely on using concrete objects or pictures to help conceptualize and solve a problem. Mathematically proficient students check their answers to problems using a different method, and they continually ask themselves, "Does this make sense?" They can understand the approaches of others to solving complex problems and identify correspondences between different approaches.

Unit 1 Lessons 8, 9, 10, 18

Unit 2 Lessons 1, 3, 5, 6, 8, 10, 13, 15, 17, 20

Unit 3 Lessons 1, 4, 7, 16, 21

Unit 4 Lessons 2, 3, 4, 5, 6, 9, 10, 12, 14, 15, 21, 22

Unit 5 Lessons 1, 2, 4, 5, 10, 15, 16, 19, 21, 22, 23

MP.2 Reason abstractly and quantitatively.

Mathematically proficient students make sense of quantities and their relationships in problem situations. They bring two complementary abilities to bear on problems involving quantitative relationships: the ability to *decontextualize*—to abstract a given situation and represent it symbolically and manipulate the representing symbols as if they have a life of their own, without necessarily attending to their referents—and the ability to *contextualize*, to pause as needed during the manipulation process in order to probe into the referents for the symbols involved. Quantitative reasoning entails habits of creating a coherent representation of the problem at hand; considering the units involved; attending to the meaning of quantities, not just how to compute them; and knowing and flexibly using different properties of operations and objects.

Unit 1 Lessons 6, 11, 14, 16, 18

Unit 2 Lessons 2, 4, 9, 20

Unit 3 Lessons 1, 3, 4, 10, 11, 12, 14, 21

Unit 4 Lessons 1, 2, 5, 6, 7, 9, 12, 16, 17, 18, 19, 22

Unit 5 Lessons 7, 15, 17, 18, 20, 23

MP.3 Construct viable arguments and critique the reasoning of others.

Mathematically proficient students understand and use stated assumptions, definitions, and previously established results in constructing arguments. They make conjectures and build a logical progression of statements to explore the truth of their conjectures. They are able to analyze situations by breaking them into cases, and can recognize and use counterexamples. They justify their conclusions, communicate them to others, and respond to the arguments of others. They reason inductively about data, making plausible arguments that take into account the context from which the data arose. Mathematically proficient students are also able to compare the effectiveness of two plausible arguments, distinguish correct logic or reasoning from that which is flawed, and—if there is a flaw in an argument—explain what it is. Elementary students can construct arguments using concrete referents such as objects, drawings, diagrams, and actions. Such arguments can make sense and be correct, even though they are not generalized or made formal until later grades. Later, students learn to determine domains to which an argument applies. Students at all grades can listen or read the arguments of others, decide whether they make sense, and ask useful questions to clarify or improve the arguments.

Unit 1 Lessons 4, 6, 10, 15, 18

Unit 2 Lessons 1, 4, 9, 16, 17, 18, 19, 20

Unit 3 Lessons 1, 2, 3, 4, 6, 7, 8, 9, 10, 11, 12, 13, 18, 19, 21

Unit 4 Lessons 1, 8, 9, 11, 13, 14, 17, 19, 21, 22

Unit 5 Lessons 1, 2, 6, 8, 12, 13, 14, 16, 17, 21, 22, 23

MP.4 Model with mathematics.

Mathematically proficient students can apply the mathematics they know to solve problems arising in everyday life, society, and the workplace. In early grades, this might be as simple as writing an addition equation to describe a situation. In middle grades, a student might apply proportional reasoning to plan a school event or analyze a problem in the community. By high school, a student might use geometry to solve a design problem or use a function to describe how one quantity of interest depends on another. Mathematically proficient students who can apply what they know are comfortable making assumptions and approximations to simplify a complicated situation, realizing that these may need revision later. They are able to identify important quantities in a practical situation and map their relationships using such tools as diagrams, two-way tables, graphs, flowcharts and formulas. They can analyze those relationships mathematically to draw conclusions. They routinely interpret their mathematical results in the context of the situation and reflect on whether the results make sense, possibly improving the model if it has not served its purpose.

Unit 1 Lessons 2, 3, 8, 9, 11, 12, 13, 14, 17, 18

Unit 2 Lessons 1, 10, 11, 14, 17, 19, 20

Unit 3 Lessons 1, 4, 7, 21, 21

Unit 4 Lessons 2, 4, 6, 8, 12, 14, 20, 21, 22

Unit 5 Lessons 3, 4, 5, 6, 7, 9, 10, 11, 12, 13, 19, 23

MP.5 Use appropriate tools strategically.

Mathematically proficient students consider the available tools when solving a mathematical problem. These tools might include pencil and paper, concrete models, a ruler, a protractor, a calculator, a spreadsheet, a computer algebra system, a statistical package, or dynamic geometry software. Proficient students are sufficiently familiar with tools appropriate for their grade or course to make sound decisions about when each of these tools might be helpful, recognizing both the insight to be gained and their limitations. For example, mathematically proficient high school students analyze graphs of functions and solutions generated using a graphing calculator. They detect possible errors by strategically using estimation and other mathematical knowledge. When making mathematical models, they know that technology can enable them to visualize the results of varying assumptions, explore consequences, and compare predictions with data. Mathematically proficient students at various grade levels are able to identify relevant external mathematical resources, such as digital content located on a website, and use them to pose or solve problems. They are able to use technological tools to explore and deepen their understanding of concepts.

Unit 1 Lessons, 14, 18

Unit 2 Lessons 4, 9, 19, 20

Unit 3 Lessons 5, 8, 9, 13, 20, 21

Unit 4 Lessons 5, 7, 9, 14, 20, 21, 22

Unit 5 Lessons 5, 6, 10, 19, 23

MP.6 Attend to precision.

Mathematically proficient students try to communicate precisely to others. They try to use clear definitions in discussion with others and in their own reasoning. They state the meaning of the symbols they choose, including using the equal sign consistently and appropriately. They are careful about specifying units of measure, and labeling axes to clarify the correspondence with quantities in a problem. They calculate accurately and efficiently, express numerical answers with a degree of precision appropriate for the problem context. In the elementary grades, students give carefully formulated explanations to each other. By the time they reach high school they have learned to examine claims and make explicit use of definitions.

Unit 1 Lessons 1, 2, 3, 5, 6, 7, 10, 11, 12, 13, 14, 15, 16, 17, 18

Unit 2 Lessons 1, 3, 4, 5, 6, 7, 8, 9, 10, 11, 12, 13, 14, 15, 17, 18, 19, 20

Unit 3 Lessons 1, 2, 3, 4, 5, 6, 8, 9, 10, 11, 12, 13, 14, 15, 17, 19, 20, 21

Unit 4 Lessons 1, 3, 4, 5, 7, 8, 9, 10, 11, 12, 13, 14, 15, 17, 18, 19, 20, 21, 22

Unit 5 Lessons 2, 6, 7, 9, 10, 11, 13, 15, 16, 17, 19, 20, 21, 22, 23

MP.7 Look for and make use of structure.

Mathematically proficient students look closely to discern a pattern or structure. Young students, for example, might notice that three and seven more is the same amount as seven and three more, or they may sort a collection of shapes according to how many sides the shapes have. Later, students will see 7×8 equals the well remembered $7 \times 5 + 7 \times 3$, in preparation for learning about the distributive property. In the expression $x^2 + 9x + 14$, older students can see the 14 as 2×7 and the 9 as $2 + 7$. They recognize the significance of an existing line in a geometric figure and can use the strategy of drawing an auxiliary line for solving problems. They also can step back for an overview and shift perspective. They can see complicated things, such as some algebraic expressions, as single objects or as being composed of several objects. For example, they can see $5 - 3(x - y)^2$ as 5 minus a positive number times a square and use that to realize that its value cannot be more than 5 for any real numbers x and y.

Unit 1 Lessons 1, 4, 5, 6, 7, 8, 9, 10, 17, 18

Unit 2 Lessons 2, 3, 4, 5, 6, 7, 8, 12, 13, 14, 16, 20

Unit 3 Lessons 2, 3, 5, 6, 7, 8, 9, 10, 11, 15, 16, 17, 21

Unit 4 Lessons 1, 2, 4, 5, 6, 7, 8, 9, 11, 12, 13, 14, 15, 16, 20, 21, 22

Unit 5 Lessons 3, 6, 7, 9, 11, 12, 13, 14, 15, 17, 18, 20, 23

MP.8 Look for and express regularity in repeated reasoning.

Mathematically proficient students notice if calculations are repeated, and look both for general methods and for shortcuts. Upper elementary students might notice when dividing 25 by 11 that they are repeating the same calculations over and over again, and conclude they have a repeating decimal. By paying attention to the calculation of slope as they repeatedly check whether points are on the line through (1, 2) with slope 3, middle school students might abstract the equation $(y - 2)/(x - 1) = 3$. Noticing the regularity in the way terms cancel when expanding $(x - 1)(x + 1)$, $(x - 1)(x^2 + x + 1)$, and $(x - 1)(x^3 + x^2 + x + 1)$ might lead them to the general formula for the sum of a geometric series. As they work to solve a problem, mathematically proficient students maintain oversight of the process, while attending to the details. They continually evaluate the reasonableness of their intermediate results.

Unit 1 Lessons 4, 7, 10, 11, 14, 17, 18

Unit 2 Lessons 16, 19, 20

Unit 3 Lessons 4, 5, 6, 7, 8, 9, 10, 12, 13, 14, 15, 17, 18, 19, 20, 21

Unit 4 Lessons 5, 6, 7, 9, 13, 15, 22

Unit 5 Lessons 15, 16, 17, 18, 20, 23

Index

Index (continued)

© Houghton Mifflin Harcourt Publishing Company